Religion After Science

In this provocative work, J. L. Schellenberg addresses those who, influenced by science, take a negative view of religion, thinking of it as outmoded if not decadent. He promotes the view that transcendently oriented religion is developmentally immature, showing the consilience of scientific thinking about deep time with his view. From this unique perspective, he responds to a number of influential cultural factors commonly thought to spell ill for religion, showing the changes – changes favorable to religion – that are now called for in how we understand them and their proper impact. Finally, he provides a defense for a new and attractive religious humanism that benefits from, rather than being hindered by, religious immaturity. In Schellenberg's view, religion can and should become a human project as monumental as science.

J. L. Schellenberg is Professor of Philosophy at Mount Saint Vincent University. His work was honored by a special issue of the Cambridge journal *Religious Studies* in 2013.

CAMBRIDGE STUDIES IN RELIGION, PHILOSOPHY, AND SOCIETY

Series Editors

Paul Moser, *Loyola University Chicago*
Chad Meister, *Bethel College*

This is a series of interdisciplinary texts devoted to major-level courses in religion, philosophy, and related fields. It includes original, current, and wide-spanning contributions by leading scholars from various disciplines that (a) focus on the central academic topics in religion and philosophy, (b) are seminal and up-to-date regarding recent developments in scholarship on the various key topics, and (c) incorporate, with needed precision and depth, the major differing perspectives and backgrounds – the central voices on the major religions and the religious, philosophical, and sociological viewpoints that cover the intellectual landscape today. Cambridge Studies in Religion, Philosophy, and Society is a direct response to this recent and widespread interest and need.

Recent Books in the Series

Roger Trigg
Religious Diversity: Philosophical and Political Dimensions

John Cottingham
Philosophy of Religion: Towards a More Humane Approach

William J. Wainwright
Reason, Revelation, and Devotion: Inference and Argument in Religion

Harry J. Gensler
Ethics and Religion

Fraser Watts
Psychology, Religion, and Spirituality: Concepts and Applications

Gordon Graham
Philosophy, Art, and Religion: Understanding Faith and Creativity

Keith Ward
The Christian Idea of God: A Philosophical Foundation for Faith

Timothy Samuel Shah and Jack Friedman
Homo Religiosus? Exploring the Roots of Religion and Religious Freedom in Human Experience

Sylvia Walsh
Kierkegaard and Religion: Personality, Character, and Virtue

Roger S. Gottlieb
Morality and the Environmental Crisis

Religion After Science

The Cultural Consequences of
Religious Immaturity

J. L. SCHELLENBERG
Mount Saint Vincent University

CAMBRIDGE
UNIVERSITY PRESS

CAMBRIDGE
UNIVERSITY PRESS

University Printing House, Cambridge CB2 8BS, United Kingdom

One Liberty Plaza, 20th Floor, New York, NY 10006, USA

477 Williamstown Road, Port Melbourne, VIC 3207, Australia

314–321, 3rd Floor, Plot 3, Splendor Forum, Jasola District Centre,
New Delhi – 110025, India

79 Anson Road, #06-04/06, Singapore 079906

Cambridge University Press is part of the University of Cambridge.

It furthers the University's mission by disseminating knowledge in the pursuit of
education, learning, and research at the highest international levels of excellence.

www.cambridge.org
Information on this title: www.cambridge.org/9781108499033
DOI: 10.1017/9781108614832

First published 2019

Printed and bound in Great Britain by Clays Ltd, Elcograf S.p.A.

A catalogue record for this publication is available from the British Library.

Library of Congress Cataloging-in-Publication Data
Names: Schellenberg, J. L., 1959– author.
Title: Religion after science : the cultural consequences of religious immaturity /
J. L. Schellenberg, Mount St Vincent University, Halifax, Nova Scotia.
Description: New York: Cambridge University Press, 2019. |
Series: Cambridge studies in religion, philosophy, and society |
Includes bibliographical references and index.
Identifiers: LCCN 2019000709 | ISBN 9781108499033 (hardback) |
ISBN 9781108713078 (paperback)
Subjects: LCSH: Religion and science. | Geological time. | Evolution.
Classification: LCC BL240.3.S34455 2019 | DDC 201/.65–dc23
LC record available at https://lccn.loc.gov/2019000709

ISBN 978-1-108-49903-3 Hardback
ISBN 978-1-108-71307-8 Paperback

For Regina

Contents

Contents

Acknowledgments

This book draws on what I've learned over the years in other writing projects, so I really ought to be thanking again everyone who helped me with them. Consider it done. It also draws, in a few places, on those past projects themselves. A version of Chapter 2 appeared as an article in the online magazine *Aeon*. And Chapters 4 and 6 contain material reprinted from "The Retrospective Mode" and "The Prospective Mode," respectively, in my book *The Wisdom to Doubt: A Justification of Religious Skepticism* (Cornell University Press, 2007). This material is used by permission of the publisher, Cornell University Press. I am grateful to Cornell for allowing me to reuse this material.

Many talented and professional people at Cambridge University Press, including the Press's philosophy editor, Robert Dreesen, worked on this book; and the questions and (sometimes inadvertent) suggestions of three anonymous referees, chosen by the Press, made for important improvements. Chad Meister and Paul Moser, editors of the Cambridge series this book joins, were unfailingly supportive, courteous, and prompt in responding to my queries. I am grateful to you all.

I owe the phrase '10,000-year test' to Philip Clayton, who used it while discussing my ideas in a talk at a Claremont conference back in 2011. I instantly liked it, and he instantly said yes when I asked whether I might use it myself, giving to it my own meaning(s). I thanked him then, and I thank him again now.

Above all, I thank my wife, Regina, to whom this book is dedicated with the greatest affection. I have the usual reasons for gratitude afforded by Regina's excellent ear and insightful comments on my ideas, as well as her abiding love and support. I also have the unusual reason that comes from her physical absence for two weeks in July of 2017, when she was traveling on the other side of the country with a daughter's family. It was then, to distract myself from missing her (it's a big country!), that I resolved to put together a book I'd been thinking about. I gave all my attention to this project. And a solid first draft was complete when she returned. Thanks, Regina!

Prologue: The 10,000-Year Test

Until little more than 200 years ago, almost everyone who contemplated the history of humanity went back only a few thousand years in time. People who entertained thoughts about the future regarded the end of the human story as nearer than the beginning. Those doing science or philosophy or commenting on religion imagined such activities to be nearing – or to have crossed – the finish line. Then came the discovery of deep geological time and evolution ... And virtually nothing changed.

As it happens, we human beings are not very good at bringing what we've learned about big temporal facts into conversation with our personal and cultural concerns. Sure, having taken a science class or two, we can rattle off geological eras taking us millions of years into the past: Cenozoic, Mesozoic, and Paleozoic. And although we haven't thought about it a lot, we'll nod knowingly when told that life on Earth, maybe including human life, has millions of years left to go – that much of the story of evolution is not yet written. But most of us haven't managed to make our everyday, lived understanding of human identity and human activity *line up* with these temporal facts. Even scientists have trouble with this.

Now, it's not as though one can immediately infer anything of interest about the status of cultural activities such as philosophy, science, and religion from the depth of the future and the shallowness of our past. It's more a matter of how an old orientation, grounded in a radically mistaken picture of time, has managed to persist and is restricting our imaginations, preventing us from even considering some pretty important and also quite live possibilities about the scale of successful inquiry and the modesty of our present attainments. In particular, it's a matter of us still being closed to some pretty important *developmental* possibilities that, 150 years after Darwin, should be wide open and familiar.

This shortcoming is more evident in some areas than in others. In this book I aim to help us correct it in an area where it seems to me especially glaring and egregious, that of human religion. The book explores and defends, in relation to a robust idea of religious transcendence, a developmental approach comfortable with temporal immensities (Chapters 1–5), setting out the often remarkable consequences of the conclusions this approach supports (Chapters 6–10). As compared with my previous work on related topics, it probes deeper on development and developmental immaturity, applying the results more widely. And with this distinctive developmental alternative in hand, it uncovers new results on the possibility of a religious humanism and in relation to the science and religion debate. In the rest of this prologue I want to warm us up for the exertions to come with a little test – call it the *10,000-year test*.

In the context of evolution, 10,000 years is not a lot of time. Even in the context of hominin evolution it's not. Mammal species – and hominins, of course, are mammals – survive on average for a million years or so. Some previous hominin species have endured for more than a million years. Take *Homo erectus*, for example. Our own species, *Homo sapiens*, has been around for about 300,000 years so far. Suppose we make it to the million-year mark – a result that's certainly not inevitable but, especially given the unique power of our technologies, hardly inconceivable either. Then the next 10,000 years amounts to only a small fraction, a mere 1/70th, of the time remaining for cultural and perhaps biological evolution to keep on changing us, what we do, and also what we *can* do.

Think of those points as evolutionary parameters for the 10,000-year test. Meditate on them a bit. Then, to begin the test itself, consider several topics of human inquiry, divided into the following four categories. Please do your best, for now, to ignore the *labels* associated with inquiry in these regions of thought that are likely to pop into your head:

(1) The individual and communal behaviors that best contribute to a productive peace and social harmony.

(2) What most fundamentally belongs to the natural world or nature, and how, at bottom, nature is structured.

(3) What is most fundamentally real, how we ought to live, and how we can know anything about such things, if we can.

(4) Whether there is or isn't <u>something beyond nature</u> that in a positive way matters for us, and, if so, what it is like.

Once you've carefully considered points (1)–(4), my test invites you to ask yourself the following question: *For which of these four categories is it most likely that at least 10,000 years of further inquiry will be needed?* A possible shortcut here is this: Ask yourself which of the associated forms of inquiry is most ambitious.

OK, time's up. Which of the four is most likely to require another 10,000 years? I expect you won't find it easy to say. (1) is just about us and thus narrower than (2), which concerns all of nature. But depending on what you say about (4), what you need to know about (1) might also go deeper than nature. (3) seems to set us a task that could hardly be finished before we had results on (1) and (2). But at the same time the identification of *any* of these inquiries as properly completed might presuppose that we'd handled the last part of (3). (4) seems unlikely to be dealt with before work on the first part of (3) is at least well underway, and it might also require us to have advanced pretty far with (2). Particular ways in which there could be a reality beyond nature may come to mind when thinking about (4), but without further information than work on (2) affords – and given that we ourselves are part of nature – we could hardly rule out lots of possibilities, needing at some point to be taken into account, that no one has yet thought of. By the same token, realities beyond nature might matter for us positively in ways we can't now imagine.

The right response to the test's first question, it appears, is this: *It's not at all obvious* which of the four is most likely to require another 10,000 years of inquiry, and in fact any of the four might call for that much more work.

Let's suppose this is true and move on to part two of the test. It involves a question that I think you'll find it much easier to handle: *For which of the four categories are people most inclined to behave as though there is no need for a* single *further year of inquiry, let alone 10,000 – that is, to treat inquiry as already complete?*

It's all right if at this point we allow those labels I earlier asked you to ignore back into our thoughts and into the discussion: they are, respectively, political inquiry (maybe with a dash of ethics), scientific inquiry, philosophical inquiry, and religious inquiry. And I expect you'll agree that the right answer to our new question has obviously got to be (4), whose associated area of inquiry is religious. People can see how complicated matters are in (1)–(3), at least when they see that (1) is about more than just which political party is best. But when it comes to (4), they've got it all figured out! Or so most suppose. For almost everyone is either a convinced believer in the existence of a transcendent reality – a reality beyond nature – that's in some way good for human life or a convinced denier of the same. And almost all convinced believers think they know just what this transcendent reality is like and what is the mode of 'positive mattering' to be associated with it, if any is. Many are certain, for example, that it's a person (or Person) who created the world and loves us. Some will add that this Person became a human being in Jesus of Nazareth and did various things in the ancient Middle East that exhibited its friendliness.

Now, the disparity that has opened up here, the gap between how much extra inquiry we can see (4) may well require, when thinking carefully and as much as possible impartially, and how much inquiry most of us are prepared to give it, is an interesting one. I think it calls for some inquiry of its own. Let's gather together everything we humans have been doing in the religious dimension of life, including in particular everything that can be seen as explicitly or implicitly concerned with satisfying ourselves about the topics of (4) above, under this label: *the religion project*. The special inquiry I've just mentioned should address at least the following questions. Have we maybe been going about the religion project the wrong way, with presuppositions and prejudices rather than careful thinking and definite results? It sure looks as though most of us have been assuming that the religion project has already reached maturity. But is our species instead still quite religiously *im*mature – and kept in this condition in part, ironically, by the prevalent assumption of maturity? And what would be the consequences for our culture's engagement with religion and religious possibilities if that were so?

This book explores these questions. By the end of it, I hope to have convinced every truth-loving observer who grapples with these matters alongside me that the religion project is indeed immature and should be given more time – another 10,000 years or more, if need be. (And with that our 10,000-year test morphs into a test of *religion* that's 10,000 years long.)

I'm especially concerned to address those who take a negative view of religion, often at least in part on the basis of scientific considerations. In the late nineteenth century, the theologian and philosopher Friedrich Schleiermacher addressed a book to what he called religion's "cultured despisers." The number of religion's cultured despisers has only grown since then, and this book in its own way addresses them, along with others among the so-called Nones (people who place a checkmark by 'None' when asked to state their religion). Many people think that human religion as we have generally known it, *transcendently oriented* religion, is on the way out. Moreover, they view its demise as a good thing. But with sensitivity to deep time, and by taking developmental ideas right into religious precincts instead of reverently leaving them outside religion's door, we will be led to the discovery that, when it comes to religious matters, our species is still developmentally quite immature. More precisely, *the religion project* is immature.

This may seem like something that in its own way is a negative result for religion. But as we'll see, by offering a new framework for our thinking, it's a result that in fact, somewhat paradoxically, allows religion to leap ahead, socially and culturally. What religion may yield, the forms it can take, how impressively rational it can be, who can be religious, how religion is related to other stances such as naturalism and atheism and humanism, and how it is related to science – our perspective on all these things will change, so I'll argue, and in ways that are surprisingly good for robust, transcendently oriented religion and also for the future of human life, once our religious immaturity is discovered, understood, and accepted.

At one level, then, this book can be seen as addressing human religious immaturity and outlining its consequences for such culturally influential views as naturalism, humanism, and agnosticism. That interpretation already accommodates my subtitle. I'm going to close this prologue with a few words about my title. *Religion After Science*: What's that all about?

I've already mentioned that I'll be considering how the relations between science and religion are affected when one adopts the new developmental perspective. It's only *after science* that this can become a question for us, so I suppose one might already see a connection to my title here. But it's not a particularly important connection in the context of this book's reasoning. Indeed, culturally important but erroneous views about science and religion are discussed in this book mainly because, like culturally important but erroneous views about naturalism and humanism and agnosticism, they are diagnosable *as* erroneous on the strength of the immaturity view. We've also already noted how ideas championed by science – ideas about development, evolution, and time – will help to shape the new perspective, including its emphasis on immaturity. It would have been a lot harder to view religious matters this way *before* science. So here we're already implicitly thinking about religion *after* science. This is indeed one thought – and a more important thought – involved in my title. But there's another thought too. This is linked to a larger 'cultural consequence' of the immaturity view than any I've yet mentioned, one for which the smaller consequences pave the way. Here it is. If what I have to say about our religious immaturity and the religion project's neglected developmental prospects is correct, then we should want to *do something about this*, giving to the religion project the dedicated sort of attention that science as a human project has already received. Religion After Science. In matters of religion we've lagged behind. But we can now make up for that. Religion can and should be the next major item on the *Homo sapiens* agenda.

I

Development and the Divine

It's interesting to think about how ideas we take for granted haven't always been lodged in someone's head. They were once in *no one's* head and had to emerge, whether among skinny humans, hulking Neanderthals, the tall but less brainy *Homo erectus*, or someone even further back in our family tree. Some individual or group had to think of using fire to serve human purposes. That was quite possibly *erectus*. Somebody dreamed up hafting a stone point onto a wooden shaft. That may have happened as far back as *Homo heidelbergensis*. And someone thought of the wheel. We humans of course were the first to *produce* a wheel, but whether we were also the first to think of one is anyone's guess.

The same kind of thing applies to every notion you can imagine. And so it is true of religious notions. Strange as it is to imagine, someone – probably members of our own species, 50,000 or more years ago – had to come up with a religious thought. Here was an original idea combining three features. First, it was about something *more* existing beyond the familiar world of fires and spears and wheels and everything else belonging to our ordinary shared experience. (After modern science tamed the familiar world and called it nature, this 'more' generally came to be viewed as something beyond nature, but when religion began, there was no science.) Second, the new thought attributed to that more a shudderingly deep inherent significance. Third, it envisaged a dramatically enhanced life for human beings – not just beyond but also in the familiar world – resulting from the right sort of connection to this unfamiliar dimension of reality.

When, in religious contexts, words such as 'more' and 'beyond' are used, the word 'transcendence' is usually close behind, invoked to express their meaning. This was already suggested in the prologue. But the same link can be made to 'shudderingly deep' and 'dramatically enhanced'; there are really three kinds of transcendence here, three ways in which religion purports to take us beyond the familiar world. The first kind, transcendent *reality*, you've probably heard mentioned in connection with religion. But for a thought to count as religious it needs to also make contact with the other two, which I'll here call transcendent *significance* and transcendent *benefit*, respectively. It may seem that these two are both about value, and they are, but to see the difference, notice that not all value has to be thought of as being for us. Value can also be conceived as inherent in something, as it is, for example, when people engage in religious worship, attributing a very great significance to what they see as transcendent. The transcendent reality *has* transcendent significance and is the *source* of transcendent benefit.

As for religion itself, we can now think of this as everything humans ever feel or do or produce – every experience and ritual and institution and tradition, and so on – that depends on our having and approving and acting on this kind of thought. It's everything in the past and present and (potentially) in the future of human life that involves really or seemingly making effective positive contact with what I'll call *triple transcendence*.

Now it's not to be expected that the first religious thought was as refined as the idea of a perfect personal God who created everything else and made fulfillment in loving relationship with God available to us – though this thought, so familiar today, clearly has the three features I've mentioned. Perhaps it was about a ghostly and ghastly realm beyond observable things, whose impressive and frightening powers needed placating to keep food plentiful or heal illness. (Dreaming, with its odd and shadowy denizens and their strange behaviors, could generate such thoughts.) But it might have been a quite different thought. Although we know how religions of the past few thousand years – Hinduism, Judaism, Christianity, Buddhism, and so on – have put flesh on the bones of triple transcendence, we have little to go on when it comes to the thinking of innumerable human beings and human communities over the last 50,000 years. And the relevant experts think religion has been around for at least as long as that. Take the colossal stone structures at Stonehenge, which many see as having religious meaning. What were the people who built them up to? What exactly were they thinking? No one knows.

But why should we suppose that it's the three features *I've* advanced that together create a religious thought? Who am I to so blithely define religiousness when – as you can tell just by leafing through one or two books on the subject – the issue of the definition of religion is actually rather controversial? I could just say that I'm the author of this new book and I get to decide how I'll be thinking about religion in it. But that response, though short, would not be sweet. So let me say a little more.

Perhaps the main thing to say is that the three-condition idea in which I'm grounding all things religious is, at least implicitly, quite widely accepted. It's not idiosyncratic but conforms closely to what many scholars of religion – including scholars of the deep evolutionary past – have found in religious thinking. Our topic is not so controversial as to preclude unanimity over significant areas. Moreover the conditions of religiousness I'm emphasizing include the aspects of it that have been most influential, which are reflected in all or most surviving religions and also philosophical discussions involving religion – aspects that even today can get people worked up and lead them to write books defending or opposing religion.

There is, it is true, an *emphasis* in what I've said and will be saying that's not as pronounced in every discussion of religion, but the basic point being emphasized is quite unoriginal too: seen from the widest perspective, human religion (together with all religion-related activity) has an important temporal component. This certainly should be examined at the level of granular detail, and when we do examine it in this way, differences among existing religious forms of life emerge that may justify speaking of religion*s*, in the plural. But it's also illuminating to zoom out, way out, and from this vantage point religion appears not as one or another tower struggling to rise high in the present but as a river running through time. Especially with the advent of evolutionary studies, it has become more common to find religion considered in this way.

Because of the extensive overlap between my view about the nature of religion and the views of other writers, if you disagree with my particular way of thinking about religion, there's still an excellent chance that what I say about it in this book will also apply to religion as you understand it. You may think there's more to religion than what I've included, but I expect you won't think there's less. Suppose, however, that you do think there's less. Perhaps, for example, you'll resist the usual tendency to identify the familiar world, which religious experiences seem to surpass, with the world of nature, explored by science. You may argue that we should instead regard it as the world of the *ordinary*: of ordinary human experiences, common to us all, of eating, drinking, working for a living, sleeping, and so on. According to my dictionary, one word for this realm of the ordinary is 'mundane,' and so instead of the transcendent, which I too am inclined to link to the surpassing of nature, we might speak of the *transmundane*, when seeking to identify what religion is about. And it's clear, on these construals, that although anything transcendent would itself be transmundane, something can be transmundane without being transcendent. Take profound aesthetic appreciation, for example, or deep wisdom.

I have argued elsewhere that the religion project, most broadly envisaged, should accept certain forms of human activity as religious that content themselves with the non-transcendently transmundane, and should include in its agenda their investigation. So I have some sympathy for such thoughts. But in my own contribution to the religion project in this book, I want to defend what I've called robust, transcendently oriented religion against its cultured detractors. We are rather far from done with such religion yet. Certainly no reason for going with transmundanity instead of transcendence that presupposed we *are* done with it would be a good reason. That is why between this book's covers the religion project, and so also religious ideas, will be construed somewhat more narrowly. If you want to take what I have to say about the immaturity of the religion project as being about just the part of the religion project that is concerned with transcendence – which is to say virtually all of it so far – that's fine by me.

HUMAN RELIGIOUS DEVELOPMENT

As my talk of a 'religion project' is meant to suggest, religious ideas – and specifically the idea of triple transcendence – ought to suggest a distinctive investigative agenda to curious humans: *Is there any such thing as a triply transcendent reality, and, if so, how should we understand its nature? Are we even able to learn anything about such profound matters?* Since many relevant possibilities will suggest themselves, and since we are limited finite beings, there is work to be done. Such work, such inquiry (and I'm taking 'inquiry' in the broadest sense; more on this below), takes time and has to grow from humble beginnings. It might grow slowly or quickly. It might experience setbacks. It might never get properly started, or just stop at some point. It is a *developmental phenomenon*.

Even though most of us, for complex and intertwined reasons of culture and psychology, may still find the concept alien, we can therefore speak of human religious development alongside human scientific development, human aesthetic development, human philosophical development, and so on. Of course, since these areas of human life are rather diverse, we might expect that development in them won't always look the same. For example, even if human religious development includes an intellectual component, the latter needn't look anything like science; its mental processes might sometimes be more like those enabling intellectual advances in art or in some other area of human experience distant from science.

But what do I mean by *development* here? Are there some general common features we can latch onto, even if the way they're realized in human life should be expected to vary?

Yes, there are. And it's important to emphasize that word 'general': when speaking of development in the present context, we're at several removes from the particular discussions of it that one finds in science – say, in evolutionary developmental biology or in developmental psychology. But that needn't be a problem. It makes sense to speak of development for human beings or their endeavors, and also of maturity and immaturity, whenever we can mark our position on a scale relative to something counting as the attainment of some relevant commodity, and whenever we can move further from or closer to this attainment. For our purposes, I propose we accept an understanding of development where the commodity is a *goal achieved* or a *capacity realized* or both. (The point of doing so will become clearer as we go along.)

There's another way, too, in which my use of the idea of development is general: when thinking about the religion project as well as the goals and capacities relevant there, I'm applying these ideas at what we might call the *macro* level, where all our human doings appear together with all our other doings in their broader natural context, exposed to us by science. The air is a bit thin up here, so it can be helpful to start by thinking of how the relevant points are illustrated at the *micro* level of individual lives and communities and their particular endeavors. In smaller human projects, one generally is aiming at some goal, and in relation to that pursuit one needs or would benefit from having some capacity or bundle of capacities. Think, for example, of an art project or an essay assignment at school. An inner-city project of community organization is another example. Such things obviously have goals. And capacities – useful, needful, and so on – can be cited in relation to these goals. For example, you need a certain degree of intelligence to write an essay successfully, and you might need to have the capacity to be very patient if you want to be a good community organizer! Furthermore, it makes sense to speak of development here, and also, by the same token, of the maturity and immaturity of such projects, because as we pursue them we are always at some location on a scale relative to the realization of such goals and capacities, and because we can move further from or closer to this attainment, whether through conscious effort or otherwise.

So, to start, we can observe that a micro-level project – and by extension (but only in that respect) anyone pursuing it – is properly judged developed or undeveloped, and so also mature or immature, by reference to how closely the relevant goal or the relevant capacity has been approached. It's possible to distinguish the realization of a project's ultimate goal from the achievement of various subsidiary goals one may need to reach along the way. Usually when I speak of a goal I'll have the ultimate goal in mind.

Although we've illustrated these points at the micro level, they are broad enough to apply at the macro level too. The goal of the religion project, as I'm understanding it, is to complete an inquiry into the topics we associated with point (4) in the prologue, concerned with the existence and nature of a transcendent (we can now say triply transcendent) reality. The relevant capacities are whatever capacities will enable us to complete this inquiry. What would count as a satisfactory completion of inquiry here might itself be regarded as a matter for inquiry. But clearly it would have to have something to do with uncovering *truths* about whether there is a triply transcendent reality and, if there is, what it is like (or determining that such truths are inaccessible to human beings). And we – collectively – can get closer to that goal or remain stationary or even fall far behind a point we had once reached. We can approach maturity or stay immature. (I'll have more to say about what immaturity specifically involves in Chapter 5, after providing evidence that this is the stage in which we're stuck.)

How exactly can we move up or down on the scale? How, in particular, can the religious dimension of human life experience development? The key is to see that we have assigned to it a fairly clear – even if daunting – *goal*. There's no mystery about how change or evolution can be progressive without some deep teleological force in nature if we have goals by which to measure our progress. Progress toward the goal of the religion project – and also toward the realization of relevant capacities, whose realization we might include among its subsidiary goals – could be made in a great variety of ways. But focusing now on the ultimate goal, it helps to notice that every new investigation of how triple transcendence might be realized can contribute to progress. The notion of a transcendent reality could have many possible realizations that are quite out of reach for us, at least as we are presently constituted, but that needn't prevent us from tackling items on the list that we do know of. If these are eliminated, we have made progress by shortening the list of possibilities. And of course we could look for information entailing that there is *no* transcendent reality, which might get us all the way to that result, and much more straightforwardly. It could also be that the right sort of multi-faceted inquiry over much time would reveal information *supporting* one or another candidate, perhaps one that emerges only in the course of inquiry, so that an advance toward enlightenment on transcendent matters is made in a more positive direction. Perhaps when a certain threshold of capacity development is crossed, everyone starts having very precise and illuminating religious experiences that over time give as much credibility to a particular picture of the divine as sensory experience is now taken to provide for our beliefs about the physical world. And so on. There are many possibilities.

Because such changes, and many others that could be imagined, would bring advances for the religion project, it makes sense to say that there is room for development in the religion project, and also, by the same token, to speak of one or another degree of maturity or immaturity for that project.

DISTINGUISHING RELIGIOUS DEVELOPMENT
FROM THE DEVELOPMENT OF RELIGION

Now, as I've already suggested, it's possible to think of this project as a project of *inquiry*. And here we're likely to encounter some criticism. It may be tempting to say that we're distorting the notion of religion by linking it in this way to inquiry. Religion, so we may hear, is more of a practical affair. It's about providing *orientation in life* for individuals and communities. By now the idea of triple transcendence has appeared among us in a dizzying array of forms, many of them incompatible with each other. If we think of religion as an attempted contribution to inquiry, that must look pretty bad. Why can't religion get its act together?! But if we think of religion properly, so this criticism goes, we won't necessarily see anything bad here at all. What matters is that people are given the distinctive sort of assistance religion can provide for negotiating their way through life. And this assistance different people and communities might very well receive by orienting themselves in relation to different and even incompatible religious ideas.

The first thing to notice as we think about how to respond to this criticism is that it has no beef with the general notion of development, even macro-level development, since a form of religion might provide orientation – the goal on this view – more or less effectively, and the human phenomenon of religion as a whole, fragmentary at first, might over time coalesce in its practical efforts, and make shorter or longer strides toward or away from macro-level practical goals.

The next thing to notice is that the practical and the intellectual aren't as easily and neatly separated as the criticism seems to assume. I have no problem with the notion of religion's role in relation to orientation in life; indeed, I'll be emphasizing related notions in subsequent chapters. But the ideas that provide orientation are usually regarded by religious people as *true*, and indeed in most cases their orientational power depends on their being regarded in this way. If you get to a state of emotional calm by praying to God, it will generally be because you believe or otherwise have faith that there really is a God who can help you. If intellectual arguments lead you to doubt or disbelieve this, you may find yourself in practical trouble. Similarly, when religious people see that other religious people are receiving nourishment from incompatible ideas, they may be led to wonder whether their own ideas really are true, and so become disoriented. In such cases, some intellectual inquiry may be needed before the good practical effects can continue.

Now, a number of thinkers have recently been suggesting that this tie between the practical and the intellectual in religion is only a contingent one. It can be unwound as we see how in various ways religious rituals which, yes, include religious ideas can be useful even when we don't any longer think about whether those ideas are true – indeed, even when we would regard them as fictitious. Prayer to an invisible friend might, given certain features of human psychology, have emotional power even when at some level we know the friend is not just invisible but nonexistent. What should we say about this?

When I hear this sort of thing I'm always at least a teensy bit suspicious that the thinkers in question have already written off notions of transcendence as objectively a failure – that it's in part *because* they have done so that this idea appeals to them. It seems to represent, for them, the only live religious alternative. But what if such an intellectual orientation only reflects how, given our culture's present condition, we are often influenced by a misplaced and indeed totally inappropriate presupposition of maturity already attained in what I'm calling the religion project, whether this be viewed as yielding a positive end result (as by religious believers) or a negative one (as by religious deniers)? What if this project is instead still in an undeveloped and quite immature condition? What if it's far too early to call it quits? What if it's wrongheaded to think of the development that's appropriate in relation to religion as an *overcoming* of robust, transcendently oriented religion by something else (for example, by science, as the nineteenth-century French philosopher Auguste Comte suggested, and many others have thought) instead of regarding it as a maturation of *transcendent religion itself*, which may result in the emergence of new and more attractive versions of robust religion in the future? As it happens, these are exactly the points I plan to defend in this book, so any critique that depends on writing off as a failure the religion project as I'm construing it can cut no ice: it assumes the very thing that is at issue.

Thus far I've responded to the critique we're considering by noting that it too can accept the basic idea of development and by arguing that the practical and the intellectual cannot be separated here as readily and uncontroversially as it supposes. A deeper point about two forms of development that need to be distinguished will complete my response.

The first of these, which I'm calling *human religious development* (or, equivalently, development in the religious dimension of human life, or the development of religious inquiry in the broadest sense, or the development of the religion project), is our focus. The second is the *development of religion*. Robust religion, in the various forms it has assumed, has its own ultimate goals, which cannot be achieved unless there is a triply transcendent reality. Relationship with God would be one example. Harmony with the Tao would be another. And religion has featured an emphasis on certain corresponding capacities, such as those associated with moral sensitivity, humility, self-awareness, and emotional adaptability. Advancements on either of these fronts – toward ultimate goals or in relation to the corresponding capacities – we might certainly regard as a kind of development. But this is not as such or specifically what I'm calling human religious development.

Now it may seem rather natural to call any such development, should it occur, religious development! But for our purposes it will be convenient to call it the development of religion instead. The term 'religious development' (along with the other terms mentioned parenthetically above) I'll reserve for the more *general* development among human beings with respect to religious matters whose profile I'm trying to raise, development which has as its goal the completion of inquiry on the matters mentioned under topic area (4) in the prologue: Whether there is or isn't something beyond nature that in a positive way matters for us (which we're now thinking of as a triply transcendent reality), and, if so, what kind of reality it is. This goal, unlike the goals of religion itself, can be pursued by the religious and the nonreligious alike. Similarly, its achievement is compatible with there being *no* triply transcendent or religious reality, and with no real development of religion ever occurring. Perhaps the negative answer on transcendence is the correct one.

Religious development, if it occurs, belongs to humanity as a whole, not just to the religious. It is *human* religious development. In this respect it is like human aesthetic development, which includes not just what you see in artists, or human scientific development, which doesn't belong exclusively to scientists. It is, again, the development of the religion project, which I've defined as including everything we humans have been doing in the religious dimension of life, including everything that can be seen as explicitly or implicitly concerned with addressing the topics of (4) above. The religion project features the railing against religion of a Richard Dawkins just as much as it does the prayers of the Pope.

What this distinction between human religious development and the development of religion allows us to say, in response to the critique we're considering, is that the inquiry on which we're focused when we discuss the religion project and the development it may or may not reveal is the sort of thing that has its own life, distinct from the life of human religious communities as such. Even if such communities were largely practical in their concerns, this would not prevent the goal of human religious development as I'm construing it – of the religion project – from requiring ardent thought and careful intellectual investigation, among other things. This goal is to be distinguished from the goals of religion, and human religious development in relation to this goal is to be distinguished from the development of religion.

But now a subtlety invites our attention, and if you get subtle enough, you'll see how it's related to my expression 'among other things' from a moment ago. Everything belonging to religion itself, and all the activities of religious people in pursuit of one or another of religion's goals, *also* belong to the religion project as we've defined it. (Of course this doesn't work the other way around.) In pursuing their own goals, religious people expose possible reasons for thinking that there is a triply transcendent reality or that there is not and possible ways of thinking about what a triply transcendent reality would be like, and so, at least implicitly, whether with positive developmental consequences or not, they offer material relevant to the goal of the religion project and thus are included in the latter's inquiry. Even if this material were largely practical or involved more in the way of cultivated experience than of dedicated thought – even if it were indeed 'other' than purely intellectual – it might contribute in this way. And here we also see why I have now and again spoken of taking the notion of inquiry relevant to the religion project 'in the broadest sense.'

The upshot is this. The critique we've been considering can in various ways be answered. And although in the present chapter we are primarily concerned with human religious development, not the development of religion, due to the subtle point just mentioned the latter and the goals appropriate to it are not simply excluded. (In Chapter 3 those goals will be getting a lot of attention in their own right.)

A RADICAL NEW APPROACH?

Such an explicitly developmental approach to our religious life as we've seen emerging here is new and may appear somewhat radical. But sometimes the radical is no more than the previously ignored. And sometimes the radical is right! That's how things are here. Or so I'm proposing.

We might have expected that after Darwin and his spectacular use of the notion of gradual change over immense periods of time and his warnings about evolved limitations, and given also all the attention that cultural evolution (as distinct from biological) and its mechanisms of change have recently been receiving, this approach I'm calling new would be old hat. But not so. Developmental ideas have made some headway in many other areas of human life, but they have never thoroughly penetrated our thinking about religion. As suggested in the prologue, we've set goals for ourselves and thought about how we might make progress toward them, recognizing that much further development may be needed to reach them, in relation to social organization, scientific understanding, and philosophical enlightenment. A more finely grained analysis would reveal that we've also done so for health and sustenance, for peace and safety, for the combatting of terrorism and environmental problems and existential threats, as well as many other things. In all these areas, we see the point of admitting ignorance and seeking understanding. But when it comes to religious possibilities, things are different.

Perhaps the psychological forces and social pressures associated with religious matters – the sort of thing that can lead to tension when the subject of religion is brought up at the supper table – are involved in the explanation of this strange fact. Perhaps the simple prejudice that can bind a believer to his belief or a disbeliever to her disbelief is to blame. For various reasons (more candidates will emerge later) it is a relatively *static* view of religion and of what needs to be done about it, investigationally speaking, that has prevailed among us. People seem generally to assume casually that religion and religion-relevant activity has got about as far as it is going to go, with religion already clearly right or wrong and the capacities that might be needed to discern this already in place. Amusingly, this seems always to have been the case. And so a clear developmental picture – the idea of a religion *project* – has generally not beckoned with any urgency. If this project is in an immature condition, it is, again, at least in part our presuppositions of *maturity* that are keeping us there.

Now, when an approach that seems sensible hasn't been tried before, we can anticipate some new and interesting results. In particular, if it should turn out that the religion project *is* in an immature condition – if this is what we have to say about the extent of its development – that would raise some very interesting prospects indeed for how we should think and otherwise behave, in relation to religious matters, in the future. As you know, I intend to defend the immaturity view. Human religious development today appears to me to be at about where the empiricist Francis Bacon found science in the early seventeenth century – and maybe even where that other Bacon fellow, Roger (who also influenced the development of what we call the scientific method), found it nearly four centuries earlier. I will have a good deal more to say about what exactly the immaturity of the religion project involves when I wrap up my defense of the immaturity view in Chapter 5. For now a pre-reflective understanding will serve, and help us keep distractions to a minimum. And then in the second half of the book, having defended and filled out the immaturity view, drawing attention to the new intellectual framework it represents, I want to display some of its striking consequences for our thinking about religion – some of those intriguing prospects I mentioned before.

The next four chapters are directed to the former task. If only because of the strong winds blowing in the other direction, I need to develop a strong cumulative case for the immaturity view. And my case begins by taking us back to the idea of deep time.

The End Is Not Near

In *Time's Arrow, Time's Cycle*, Stephen Jay Gould tells the story of one John Playfair, who in 1788 accompanied the great British geologist James Hutton to see an 'unconformity' at Siccar Point in Scotland. With the help of this geological visual – an ancient erosion surface dividing two layers of rock, one gently sloping, the other vertically tilted – Hutton explained to Playfair that the Earth is a machine ceaselessly repeating a cycle of erosion, deposition, and uplift. Playfair later wrote: "The impression made will not easily be forgotten ... Revolutions still more remote appeared in the distance of this extraordinary perspective. The mind seemed to grow giddy by looking so far into the abyss of time."

Giddy. That's how trying to penetrate 'deep time' has made people feel ever since its relatively recent discovery by science. With a little practice, one can contemplate thousands of years, but thinking in the millions is a bit like staring into a bottomless well or crevasse. No doubt this has something to do with the name 'deep time.'

By now most of us have absorbed and integrated quite a large number of facts about deep time. We acknowledge that our universe began with the big bang about 14 billion years ago. We know that our planet has 'gone cycling on,' to use Charles Darwin's phrase, for about 4.5 billion years. Darwin himself didn't know the age of the Earth, and would have been greatly relieved to hear of it, because natural selection, which he hoped he had discovered, requires hundreds of millions of years to do its creative work, to produce the vast number of forms that sprint along the Earth's surface or splash and soar in its seas and skies. To the extent that we've begun to internalize this idea of deep time, we have started to make the difficult transition from human timescales to those of science. Most of us are now able, for example, to process the idea that the evolution of our species, *Homo sapiens*, in Africa some 300,000 years ago is a comparatively recent event, coming at the end of a long period of hominin evolution involving other species with fancy names such as *Homo erectus* and *Australopithecus afarensis* – one that runs back in time at least 7 million years. And this period, considered in its entirety, is still just one small branch on the massive tree of life that's been growing on our planet for at least 3.5 billion years.

But we're a long way from seeing and internalizing what deep time means for our own hominin thinking – and this, as I will show, includes the thinking required for large human endeavors such as the religion project.

HUMAN PROJECTS IN DEEP-TIME PERSPECTIVE

You may have noticed that 50,000 years, the period, roughly, that the religion project has had so far, seems like a really long time, especially when set next to the days of our lives. The same would have to be said for other basic human projects such as those involving art, which go back even further in time, as well as philosophy and science, which occupy less time but still seem old to us. (Philosophy has been going on in the West since about 600 years before Christ. Recognizing this, we often marvel at its ancient venerability.) Our personal experience of events crammed into minutes and hours and weeks and months joined to human cognitive limitations makes it hard to think with any concreteness beyond a few hundred years. Try, for example, to picture your children (real or imagined) having children, and those children – your grandchildren – growing old and dying, leaving their own children to grow old. By the time you imagine your great-grandchildren all wrinkled and grey and maybe older than yourself in the present, living amid quite altered physical and cultural circumstances, you're probably starting to get a bit dizzy. And you haven't even made it through the next century!

So a history of 50,000 years, very naturally, seems long to us. But when thinking with the aid of science, we'll see that it isn't nearly as long as it seems. Instead of taking us anywhere near the shrouded beginnings of things, it takes us through just 1/6th of the life of our own species, *Homo sapiens*, and across only about 1/38th of the temporal expanse separating us from the beginning of *Homo erectus*, whose origin is dated to about 1.9 million years ago. It's rather hard to imagine all this, but science will properly lead you to accept it.

Now notice that, so far, we've ignored the deep future. (I did try to get you about a century and a half into the future with my thought experiment about children and grandchildren a moment ago, but despite the difficulties we discovered, that's not very deep.) Indeed, almost all references to deep time you find in books are asking us to look backward into history. In most of our talk about deep time, what we really have in mind, therefore, is the deep *past*. Every day, we're reminded that we come at the end of a long evolutionary process. I reminded you of that at the end of the previous section. There is little to stimulate the thought that we come at the very beginning of one, too. Thus even if we grasp that 50,000 years going back in time doesn't take us that far, there's little to prod us to the realization that it's not very far going forward either.

When we do start thinking about the future, it can still be difficult to get a real sense of how much of it there will be, even just for life on our planet. A billion years at least is needed to get you all the way from whatever was going on with us 50,000 years ago through the immensities of time that lie ahead for species on our planet, before the Sun's unbearable drying heat causes the evolution of life on Earth to grind to a halt. But while we know a billion years is more than 50,000 years – writing out the number we'll see there are five more zeros – how *much* more is hard for our hominin brains to take in. You'd have to cross a 50,000-year period, which to us seems immense, 20,000 *times* to reach the temporal destination of a billion years. We need to meditate on such facts. They teach us that it takes a great deal longer than one might think for intelligent life to travel any distance at all through scientific time. From this perspective all our human enterprises appear to be still quite close to their starting point. The beginning is near!

Bettering Playfair, whom we met at the beginning of this chapter, by also looking forward from where we are into the abyss of future time, imagining what yet may be, is obviously not something we're very good at. But it's something I believe we ought to deliberately try to get good at, in order to correct what amounts to an unbalanced outlook and discover our place in time. To see things as they are includes seeing them as they will be, and that means picturing ourselves and our own position in time not as coming at the end, jutting out into empty space with nothing beyond, but as tucked in with manifestations of life both behind us and ahead of us. Tucked in, just as Darwin's or Hutton's time is for us as we look back on it now. That is how things will be.

With this in mind, let's think some more about human enterprises such as those involving art and philosophy and science and religion.

Suppose all such enterprises are brought to the most profound truths and experiences available by some evolved species on our planet. (The *most profound*: not just relatively elementary findings such as evolution and deep time.) Will it be us? Think specifically of religion. Even religious people don't believe that *Homo erectus* grasped important truths about religion. So what if we don't either, but some species much further down the line, evolutionarily, gets there?

But suppose it is us. How long might that take, even assuming we put our best foot forward? We might, for example, as part of the religion project, want to give various forms of real live religion a good chance to realize their ambitions. But religious ambitions, as we'll see in the next chapter, are enormous ambitions for an evolved species. Then, too, when thinking at this fundamental level we can't assume that if there's anything corresponding to what religion is looking for, it's a *personal* being who *wants* to be found. It would be natural for creatures like us who are persons to start out thinking of the divine as a person (or as persons), thus generating the idea of a God (or gods). But this idea might indeed leave us close to the starting line or – to shift metaphors – at the very top of a bucket of ideas indicating ways in which religious notions can be formulated.

BEATING BACK OUR BIASES

The central point of this chapter is now in view: although it may seem that human enterprises such as the religion project have had lots of time to make their most impressive discoveries, a deep-time perspective, when properly internalized, will leave us quite unsure about that. Maybe scientific timescales rather than human timescales would govern any such discoveries, and we've simply failed to notice this. If so, then even if we've been doing our best – and indeed even if the brightest form of success is inevitable given the right efforts, sufficiently long sustained – intelligence on our planet may only have got started on some of its biggest quests.

But human timescales are seductive. And, as I've noted, even when we think we're taking deep time into account, our thinking tends to be unbalanced, skewed toward the past. Thus in this section I try to lay bare some of the causes of a prejudice in favor of past and present when it comes to thinking about our most preoccupying activities. Aware of how we can be prejudiced here, we'll be more likely to adjust for this.

So why is it that, after discovering the place of the Earth in the solar system, the place of the solar system in the universe, the age of the Earth, the age of the universe, and evolution by natural selection over aeons of Earth's history, we still need to be prodded to perform the simple act of turning around?

A possible reason that will come swiftly to mind is human self-preoccupation. The line of evolution reaches us, and we find it hard to imagine it moving much further. Hugely impressed with our own accomplishments, including those just listed, we give little thought to ideas no one has yet had or to species not yet a twinkle in evolution's eye. There is also a more practical reason. Most personal human goals, including altruistic ones, rise or fall over the short period of a human lifetime. And although as we pursue them we may sometimes look back – even far back – with interest, perhaps to learn from our kind's history, there is nothing in the far future that's similarly tied up with our goals. As a result, we haven't developed the habits of mind necessary to consider it carefully.

The past has another kind of allure for us, one tied closely to the way we see ourselves. When we do lift our heads from immediate human concerns and think in scientific timescales, our attention is often drawn in a special way to times gone by. As attested by hundreds of nature programs on TV, things that occurred in the recesses of evolutionary time can touch us deeply, for they affect our very sense of identity. Having discovered evolution, we now know that many secrets about who we are might be exposed by the paleoanthropologist's shovel or brush. But there is no bed of deposits where you can dig up the fossils of your descendants.

Interestingly, given the subject of this book, we might also pin some of the blame on religious scriptures such as the Bible or the Qur'an. Even if you think of them as casting a long shadow across the history of Western culture, there is no denying their powerful influence on the way that we think today. And you might have noticed that there's not much about a billion-year future in such books. They do not tell us "The beginning is near!" but rather "The end is near!" When I was a small boy, I helped my father put an actual sign at the end of our driveway that said "Jesus is coming soon." And although his brand of enthusiastic evangelicalism sponsored endless disputes with other Christians – even other evangelicals – as to how things will transpire in the near future, on the matter of whether we are living in the end times he was in lockstep with other biblical believers. If you allow for secular eschatologies, he was also in lockstep with the rest of the culture, which has by now spun out rather a large number of variations on the religious Armageddon-just-around-the-corner theme; new ones can be viewed in your local Cineplex every other week. We all want to live in the most exciting, most consequential chapter of time, it seems.

Finally, there's the simple problem of our limited imaginative power, which may indeed be pretty fundamental here, underlying some of the others. This problem is illustrated by a recent paper in *Science*, which proposed a new cognitive illusion called the end of history illusion. The illusion emerges when individuals are asked to consider whether important personal changes are still ahead of them instead of behind. As it happens, we tend to deny this. What six studies of more than 19,000 participants confirmed is that "predictors aged *a* predicted that they would change less over the next decade than reporters aged *a* + 10 years reported having changed over the same decade." As the authors of the *Science* article put it:

Although the magnitude of this end of history illusion in some of our studies was greater for younger people than for older people, it was nonetheless evident at every stage of adult life that we could analyze. Both teenagers and grandparents seem to believe that the pace of personal change has slowed to a crawl and that they have recently become the people they will remain. History, it seems, is always ending today.

The authors hazard some explanations for this phenomenon. What they say, drawing on other psychological studies, is, first, that people tend to think in a laudatory way about their own personalities, values, and preferences, and having reached such an elevated condition, are likely not to consider the possibility of change. This is not implausible, and should remind us of the point about human self-preoccupation made above. But another point the authors make is of more interest just now. *Imaginative* efforts requiring that we look ahead, they say, are harder for us, mentally, than thinking about the past, which is after all aided by *memory*:

If people find it difficult to imagine the ways in which their traits, values, or preferences will change in the future, they may assume that such changes are unlikely. In short, people may confuse the difficulty of imagining personal change with the unlikelihood of change itself.

The 'history' such studies are concerned with is of course personal history. But what if we moved things up a level or two, taking that phrase 'end of history' in its larger and more usual sense? Would we find similar illusions? I think we would. Notice that we tend to think in a laudatory way about our species, not just about ourselves personally. A species-based self-importance has to be added to any individual self-importance we may exhibit. Imagine how you would feel if you entered a room which had in it various members of previous hominin species – here's Lucy, over there is Ardi – and came to realize that their movements or sounds indicated curiosity about their environment or the world at large. Wouldn't you feel immensely superior in the relevant, intellectual respects? Wouldn't you want to be able to enlighten them? Furthermore, would it so much as cross your mind that absent from the group are representatives from a possible species 3 million years hence, as far advanced beyond ourselves as we are beyond the australopithecines, who might be able to tell *us* a thing or two? With all this self-importance, the idea that we as a species haven't yet 'arrived' in this or that respect would have to knock at your door a long time to get noticed.

But the point about our limited imaginations applies at higher levels too; being thus limited could easily contribute to a large-scale end of history illusion of the sort in question. Remember how hard it is to imagine the deep future of our species. It's a lot harder than imagining what life will be like for us, personally, in another ten years. Even the *shallow* future is challenging: who, 200 years ago, could have foreseen the iPhone? Moreover, without imaginative help, it's rather easy to conflate the edge of history, where beings in any 'present' moment find themselves, with the end. (In many ways the pinnacle of human development so far is reached in our own lifetime, and it's easy to ignore the 'so far.')

So there are all these possible and often plausible sources of a human bias in favor of focusing our thinking on past and present rather than the future. In our central human activities they operate with full force. Consider, in particular, the possibility of a large-scale end of history illusion in connection with religion. This, on reflection, will seem pretty plausible. For virtually all religious discussion and also discussion about religion presupposes that major religious developments have come to an end. What you see, so it is supposed, is very largely what you're going to get. Our religious aspirations, it is assumed, are quite fully tapped. Consequently, most of us, when thinking about religion, find ourselves looking backward, into the past, rather than both backward and forward, along a more generous line of vision that includes the future. Even prophets and reformers, aflame with the new, are looking back. It's just that, for them, the pinnacle of religious development has been reached in the very *recent* past! And it's important to see that similar thinking is found among critics of religion, who might otherwise have goaded us to take the religion project further within a more generous temporal perspective. For example, evangelicals and new atheists alike suppose that we today, at the beginning of the twenty-first century, are in a position to utter the Last Word on religious matters. Of course they disagree radically on what it should be, but they are at one in the presupposition that the history of significant religious development on our planet is over.

Now I won't be arguing that people who think about religion in the way I've just described are subject to the influence of a false scientific or metaphysical belief about the end of important religious change. It's not as obvious in this larger case as it is at the personal level that significant change is likely to continue if we live on. But we still have an important cognitive illusion. For it's being assumed that confidence about the end of religious history is warranted when this is not the case. What we have to go on simply doesn't support the widespread confidence one finds about this subject. On considering the relevant facts, such confidence will not be regarded as a soberly reasoned or reasonable response to reality but rather as manifesting a cognitive illusion – an illusion reflecting a lack of imagination, and maybe also the influence of some of the other factors mentioned above.

From the discoveries of this chapter, nothing dramatic follows about what stage the religion project is in. How much time has passed is one thing; how far we've matured is another. But having beaten back our biases on these topics, we may become more open to developmental thoughts. And, noticing how closed we were before, we may come to realize that maturity for our most profound endeavors could very well lie much further ahead than we have imagined – much further ahead than our hominin brains, until very recently, have even allowed us to imagine.

The point here is really a point about *scale*. We should remember how often humans have been mistaken on matters of scale and corrected by science. Think of errors about the size of the distances between Earth and the stars, about the size of the galaxy, about the size of the universe itself. If our relevant impulses are shaped by a love of truth, then we'll take on board the idea that where the temporal 'size' or scale of the religion project is concerned, we may well be similarly mistaken.

3

Big Ambitions

Why have I been calling the religion project a *big* project? In part, certainly, because when thinking about it, we are operating at the macro level, where it's not just what I think or feel or what's going on at the synagogue down the road that's relevant but anything that any human has ever felt or done in relation to the notion of transcendence. The religion project is a *human* project; it belongs to us all. That makes it big. But, as I've already suggested once or twice, the religion project is also big because of its *outsize ambitions*. Trying to figure out as much as you can about whether there's something more to reality than just nature – and something benign – or trying to understand the transcendent reality you already believe to be there is not very much like trying to fix your car or outfox a business rival. It's a bit more complicated. And this despite all those who think they've long been privy to such information because of what their priest or professor said or an experience they've had. (And here you can include a Sartrean sense of the absence of the divine as much as anyone's more positive religious experience.)

Because they're so large, when considering the ambitions of the religion project we are collecting information that's relevant to the question whether the religion project is still at an immature stage of development rather than already mature as many suppose. It can take a lot of time and effort to get big jobs done. And in the next chapter we'll have a look at whether our efforts have matched our ambitions. But here we just want to get a better sense of what these ambitions are and how big they are. Clearly, when talking about them we're talking about goals, such as the ultimate goal of the religion project, to which I've already alluded, and the goals of religion itself, which in Chapter 1 we found to be distinct

from but importantly related to the former goal. (Indeed, someone might
have both in view, seeing the pursuit of religious goals as serving – and
in that respect subsidiary to – the goal of the religion project.) I'm using
the word 'ambition' instead because we can always ask how ambitious
goals are, and goals that are ambitious we naturally call ambitions. Here
we're going even further and taking account of how the ambitions of the
religion project are *large* ambitions.

My main subject in this chapter will be the ambitions of religion, since,
so far, it's primarily through religious belief and practice that people
have addressed the goal of the religion project. Any progress this human
activity represents for the religion project is of course tied to progress in
the pursuit of religious ambitions, so the size of the latter is directly relevant. Here and there along the way, I'll have occasion to comment also on
the central ambition of the religion project as such, and on the ambition
to realize it by showing that there is no transcendent reality at all, which
is the other main ambition we've seen addressed in the religion project so
far. But first let's look a bit more closely at what we mean when we say
that someone's ambition is *big*.

WHAT DO WE MEAN BY 'BIG' HERE?

When we say that someone has big ambitions, what we generally mean is
that their goals are impressively sized, often relative to other things that
might have been attempted, both in terms of the *change* that would result
from success and the *resources* that would need to be marshaled to bring
it about, the procuring of which is thought to entail special *challenges*
or difficulties. Hitler's goal of world domination is a clear example.
Obviously the world would be a lot different had the Nazis won World
War II. Enormous resources were brought to bear on the task. German
financial costs alone reached at least $210.4 billion, according to a 1947
estimate. And the challenges Hitler faced are well known, as well as the
fact that they eventually became insurmountable.

All three of these things – big change, big resources, and big challenges –
will be discussed in this chapter as we consider the size of the ambitions
involved in the religion project. By addressing these aspects of their
'bigness' separately, we'll make our own task more manageable. As the
definitions of Chapter 1 help us to see, religion seeks a great enlargement
in our understanding of the world and correspondingly large practical
changes. The various religions are trying to map not just the familiar

world but also the less familiar and quite literally extraordinary regions they tell us lie beyond. As indicated when the word 'ultimate' is used to describe their concerns – as in 'ultimate reality' – the religions of today often want this map to be perfectly *comprehensive*, to convey the most deeply important insights about life, the universe, and everything. But the basic distinction between familiar and extraordinary dimensions of reality suffices to bring into view the rather large cartographical aims even of religions that don't go that far. And of course that's not all. Religions want to use that map of the extraordinary to travel into better conditions both there and here, in the familiar world, effecting whatever changes in the human condition are required to do so. These would, to say the least, be enormous changes from hunter-gatherer existence pre-religion, or indeed from any other sort of human existence outside religion's sphere of influence. And, as we'll see, the resources required and challenges incurred have to be assessed as large in size too.

We have, then, three features of 'bigness' to explore in relation to the big ambitions of religion as well as the other ambitions reflected in the religion project as we've seen it so far: big changes, big resources, and big challenges.

BIG CHANGES

People who go to church for the first time will sometimes recoil from what appears to be a rather blatant attempt to *change* them. Now if you stick around long enough to glean a second or third impression, and are lucky enough to land with less aggressive churchy types, you may sense that you're being invited to change yourself, and (so it is thought) change yourself positively, or to open yourself to being changed positively by some transcendent reality. But there's no denying that churches – and much the same thing could be said of synagogues, mosques, temples, ashrams, and so on – are in the change business.

Religion by its very nature has always been in the change business. Something in the familiar world needs alteration or reorientation in light of what the seer thinks he sees of the transcendent realm. And something must be set right or made whole. In today's religions the idea is generally that with a focus on the familiar world, or on the familiar world alone, without the perspective offered by a transcendent vision, come seductive influences that distort our picture of the world or ourselves and shrink our potential, making us less happy or less aware or less good or less free.

Notice that religion therefore does indeed want us to be inwardly changed in a big way, transformed, in some manner having psychological and social as well as moral and spiritual aspects. But to get this going in the right way and in the right direction, it must also seek broadly intellectual change. It seeks a broadened perspective that is shaped, in part, by true information about a transcendent reality and transcendent value. For anyone schooled by the familiar world alone, the shift to such a picture of things would have to mean a big change too.

We should take a moment to consider just how much is looked for here. Big and beneficial personal changes, with all their social effects, built on a radically changed understanding of the world, and of course this understanding needs to be compatible with other correct understandings – today especially in science. As suggested, not just any personal changes and understanding, however interesting, are in view: what's desired are positive personal changes of the right sort, built on a true understanding. We can make a link here to what I said in Chapter 1 about triple transcendence. Religion wants a dramatic enhancement of human life, that is, transcendent benefit, resulting from a right orientation not just to one or another transcendent idea but to transcendent *reality*.

Most religions have moreover been missionary religions, seeking to spread the good news they see as entailed by their vision as far as possible. So there's a hope that the changes described here will ultimately reach every corner of the familiar world, and bring every one of us – or at any rate all who are well disposed – into religion's friendly embrace. Neither science nor philosophy nor art nor any other basic human activity has ever sought this much change.

Some of the points I've been making apply also to the central ambition of the religion project considered as such, and to the ambitions of those who oppose religion or religious ideas. However, the former ambition might be achieved, it would call for a big shift from perspectives in which we're schooled by the familiar world to a challenging broader perspective shaped by an ardent search for true information about transcendent things. And for those who oppose religion and religious ideas, perhaps because for them nature appears to be the only reality and is enough, success would require a mental shift permitting real engagement with people of a very different mental orientation, by now instantiated in a multiplicity of forms – a shift allowing them to clearly see and properly reject what that orientation has to offer in the way of alternative ideas.

Plenty of change to go around.

BIG RESOURCES

To successfully bring about such large changes, large resources are needed. What is required? As it turns out, mainly *knowledge*, if we construe it broadly enough.

Given the third kind of transcendence we've seen to be associated with it, namely, transcendent benefit, religious success clearly requires a practical ability or know-how. Individuals and communities need to discover and internalize ways of behaving that, at the deepest level, will allow a real connection to the transcendent to be formed, with all its psychological, social, and other consequences. To achieve this, they will also need a kind of meta-level know-how: they'll need to know how to cultivate successfully a desire to behave in these ways as well as the courage needed for the most difficult religious actions. In religion as we see it now, such things as fasting, rituals and prayers of confession, as well as contemplation and meditation, are intended to exhibit these sorts of know-how. Whether these will ever actually do the trick or not, they at any rate provide examples of the sort of thing needed here.

There is of course another ability religion needs to have for success – a cognitive ability expressed in having the right beliefs. Here we're talking about knowing-*that* instead of knowing-how: knowing that the transcendent reality is of *this* kind instead of some other, and its importance and value of *this* kind instead of some other: no-self and ultimate awareness as some Buddhists have it, for example, instead of a God who loves our sinful selves as Christians say. Indeed, the know-how that the desired changes require would be dependent on knowing-that. You could try all you like to get to a heavenly relationship with God, but if your attempt is based on bad information – if, say, the Buddhists are right and there is no God – it's not going to take you where you want to go; you'll be unsuccessful.

We should notice that the cognitive abilities required here will extend beyond purely metaphysical insight, concerned with establishing the basic nature of reality. The transcendence at issue is, again, *triple* transcendence. Moral and aesthetic and other value-related cognitive performances, we should expect, will be needed too. The shaman of tribal religion was capable of such performances. Priests and mystics and artists of various kinds have also been thought to deliver them.

Philosophers who prize a narrow sort of metaphysical insight will therefore be thought rather one-sided by the religious. Those scientists who think nothing more than their own discipline is needed for a full understanding of life will seem similarly one-sided. For religious success, beauty and the good must be understood along with metaphysics. And knowledge of value acquired from music or painting may be as important as that communicated in books.

Again, parallel points apply to other ambitions of the religion project that might be mentioned here. A certain kind of know-how will be needed to truly enter the orientation of religious people by those who seek to explore that orientation and what it delivers responsibly. And knowing-that is required whenever people are sorting through transcendent possibilities, hoping to determine whether any is realized. It is certainly needed by those who wish to defend the view that the transcendent reality is *not* of this kind or *not* of that kind, or does not exist at all.

BIG CHALLENGES

So big changes sought and big resources required. But rather large and serious challenges stand in the way. Success in science is a tall order. Philosophical success is a really tall order. But religious success is arguably the tallest. And given the connections we've noted between other ways of succeeding in the religion project and religious success, those other ways are not much less tall. Of course we could have a special talent for religion or religion-related inquiry, or special help for attaining its goals. We might then already be really advanced, both cognitively and practically, in ways relevant to the ambitions we are considering. And if that were so, then realizing them might be well within our reach, and we wouldn't rightly think of the challenges as very severe. The religion project might be a snap, as apparently many think it is. But before considering some views that try to move us in this direction, let's pause to remind ourselves of a few relevant facts.

To be religiously advanced, we'd have to be good at things in ways that are rather different from the ways in which humans most conspicuously are good at things. What we're obviously good at is devising solutions to practical problems and inventing ever more sophisticated ways of satisfying desires elicited by the familiar world. Our innovative powers help to explain why *we* survived when the weather changed sharply some 40,000 years ago though the hapless Neanderthals didn't. And of course by now we have not just fire and the spear and the wheel but the iPhone and GPS and gene therapy and nuclear bombs. Such developments have been spurred in part by our biggest invention: science. But notice how all of this keeps us squarely planted in the familiar world, the world of ordinary shared experience, which, more and more, we are coming to understand and manipulate in service of the most demanding human needs and wants. To invent the iPhone, Steve Jobs and his team didn't talk to God; they talked to scientists and engineers – latter-day fire-builders and wheel-makers.

Success in religion too would involve a practical ability or know-how, given the third kind of transcendence I've associated with it. But just think about the sort of thing religion requires us to be able to know how to do: make a positive connection to something rather different from anything in the familiar world, maybe even entirely non-physical and non-material, and in any case quite beyond the reach of science. If what we're most obviously good at is science, and religion aims at something beyond its reach, mightn't that aim be a bit difficult to achieve?

And while we're at it, we should remember the other kind of ability religion would need to have – a cognitive ability expressed in knowing that the transcendent reality is of *this* kind instead of some other, and its importance and value of *that* kind instead of some other. Religion hopes to access transcendent and maybe even ultimate truths about what is real and what matters. Thus we can make the point about science in another way: If the kind of knowing-that which we're good at is the sort delivered by science, theoretical and applied, which allows us to know that some detailed portion of the physical world is or can be configured one way rather than another but tells us nothing about things that would have to be radically different if they existed at all, then religious knowing-that looks like it might be rather challenging for human beings, a bit of an uphill climb, to say the least.

Maneuvering adroitly enough among religious notions to show that *none* is realized or that such results can never be reached by humans is going to be challenging for similar reasons. Of course an opponent of religious ideas might try to sidestep such maneuvering by arguing that nature is all there is and *inferring* that nothing transcendent is real. But the worry then, given the intellectual specialty of humans, must be that we haven't given religious possibilities a fair shake. Until we've worked to thoroughly understand a representative set of such possibilities, how can we be sure that we're not just making reality fit what we're familiar with, like someone with his head bound so he can only look forward who thinks there's nothing behind him or at either side?

Religious people will probably think that they have the advantage here. Whether they be Buddhist or Christian or Hindu or reliant on some other strand of existing human religion, they are likely to find congenial the following objection to the line of thought I've been developing. "Religious or spiritual knowing – whether knowing-that or knowing-how – isn't something one has to figure out how to acquire through the application of some natural human cleverness. No, it has been or can be given to us from beyond the familiar world by ——." Fill the blank with some source of religious revelation: God or the Tao or the Buddha-nature or something else along those lines.

We should consider this objection carefully. Here, where my concern is with the tall order of religious success, we don't need to go into the details of any religion's particular offer but can take the point of the objection more abstractly, as suggesting a possible way of keeping on top of challenges like those I've been describing to which religion uniquely has access. The transcendent reality itself can help us! It can help us both through a revelation of religious truths and by reaching out to us from its side – preventing us from having to figure out how to get across that big gap between the familiar world and transcendent things all by ourselves.

Now, this way of putting the thought here might still seem to be pre-judging the issue of what the transcendent facts, if there were any, would be like, by assuming the existence of a personal God who generously and graciously tells us truths and (metaphorically) offers us a helping hand. But maybe – just maybe – we can take its language as even more deeply figurative without losing a substantial religious response to the alleged challenges of the religion project. The suggestion, we may suppose, is that the transcendent facts simply are such that, in one way or another, whether through personal divine grace or something else, under realiz-able circumstances the needed knowledge will bloom in human hearts and minds.

Such an appeal to revelation might be thought to preserve an appro-priate humility for religious persons as well as for any associated form of religion in the face of cognitive challenges. But, sadly, it does no such thing. The idea that knowledge of one kind or another is given to human beings from a transcendent source is itself something human beings are claiming to know! So the question about religious knowledge has not been satisfactorily answered. It has only been made to rise again, at a slightly different point: How do you know *that*? And we can see that our worrying observations above are waiting and ready to be applied specif-ically to this revelation claim. The nature of a revelatory 'power beyond' would share in the nature of transcendent facts, should there be any. So what makes us think, given what we know of their profundity and our own evolved competencies, that we would be able to fathom its nature?

For that matter, why think that the kinds of facts it would have to reveal could be *held* by a human mind?

Perhaps the best religious response, if the aim is to blunt my point about natural human competencies, will put the basic point about revelation in terms of *religious experience*: "One night God's sustaining presence became very real to me"; "After long contemplation I suddenly saw the Truth." Religious experience might seem to be a special source of distinctively religious information, unique to the religious realm, which provides religion with its *own* credentials and competencies, and moreover affords powerful psychological support for its enterprises.

That religious experience affords a good deal of psychological support for religious enterprises is not to be denied. But here we need to recall that the religious want not just to feel good about where they are – to have some sort of positive psychological result from their activities – but to have this *while being on the right track*, in fact attuned to a transcendent dimension of reality. And there is a reason for doubt about the capacity of religious experience, as we have known it thus far, to provide such assurance for the discerning.

Here it's natural to begin by wondering about some pretty obvious differences between religious experience and the ordinary sensory experience that fills every waking moment and feeds science. For example, it may seem that, like sensory experiences, religious experiences with detailed intellectual content should be widely shared and capable of being intentionally repeated and corroborated – which they are not – if they are to be viewed as reliable truth-presenters. But a persuasive reply to this sort of objection can be found in the work of the late twentieth-century American philosopher William P. Alston, who suggested that it reflects prejudice and an arbitrary chauvinism. Why suppose that all reliable and truth-presenting experience has to be like sensory experience? Why couldn't there be many different kinds of experience, all capable of presenting truth in ways appropriate to what they are the experience of? As we were just noting, if there are religious facts, they are going to be rather different from ordinary facts in the familiar world. So why not admit that the way to experience them, if there were one, would be different from ordinary experience?

This sort of move may deal with one problem for religious experience as a reliable source of information about transcendent things. But there is a way of deepening the problem that even Alston realized it would be challenging to deal with properly. Instead of saying only that religious experience is frequently non-shared, emphasize that it is often *contradicted* – in the sense that what one person says on the basis of her religious experience is often ruled out by what others say on the basis of theirs. This, indeed, is how we got the many different and conflicting religious traditions of the world today: Buddhists, Hindus, Christians, Jews, Muslims, Jains, and other religious people are constantly contradicting each other in the details of what they say about the transcendent on the basis of their special experiences. If religious experience were a reliable source of information about worlds beyond, shouldn't we find that people from around the familiar world – at any rate decent, careful, and conscientious people – have religious experiences and make religious claims that are mutually reinforcing and complementary rather than contradictory and conflicting? Since there are contradictions instead, we already know that some decent, careful, and conscientious people are deceived by their religious experiences: when two claims contradict, one has got to be false. That's as clear as two plus two equaling four. So why not him, or her … or *me*? If we add 'intellectually humble' to 'decent, careful, and conscientious' then anyone with these qualities who knows about the conflicts among religious experiences is going to say, if she has a religious experience herself, that its intellectual content is open to question – certainly on details. Even if, for example, she finds herself involuntarily believing that Jesus is Lord of All when she comes out of the experience, she will not expect this to be information that should help her a lot when trying to make a case for her own view in the context of the religion project.

Now, as a religious person who has religious experiences, you might hope to maneuver yourself into a better position on this issue by getting to know all the different ways of being religious, as well as representative practitioners from the different streams of religious life and their brands of religious experience, really well, and through appropriate inquiry determining conclusively who – if anyone – is really in touch with a transcendent reality. But now look at all the *new* challenges we've introduced. (Some of the old ones remain: it may be an uphill climb, given the natural talents of *Homo sapiens*, to pull off that last move.) Alston suggests that what's needed is a massive transreligious "system of overriders," a shared body of religious beliefs and beliefs about religion that we can appeal to when judging certain experiences unreliable, which functions much as does our large body of shared beliefs drawn from sensory experience when it comes to disputed claims about the familiar world. It might be a bit of a job to get such an overrider system, he reasonably suggests. Indeed, saying so is just another way of saying what we said earlier about our one-sided talents. And we haven't even mentioned the *new forms of religious experience* that may keep emerging as time goes on – or as we engage in efforts like this – and the need to also figure out what to do about *non-* or *anti-*religious experiences such as the Sartrean experience mentioned at the beginning of this chapter.

The upshot is that the big challenges faced by religious ambitions don't get a lot smaller when we consider the appeal to religious experience.

DO BIG AMBITIONS NEED DEEP TIME?

We've seen that there are big challenges in the way of mustering the big resources needed to make big religious or religion-related change happen. But how much time would all of this take? Might the amount of time required be big too?

Here we see how this chapter, with its emphasis on the size of the religion project's ambitions, is related to the previous chapter, which sensitized us to the possible relevance of deep time to human activities viewed from a macro-level perspective. We know that it often takes more time to handle big ambitions than small ones. In Chapter 2 I mentioned in passing how religion-related ambitions are especially big. Now we have the evidence. So the possibility that deep time might be especially relevant to religion should be getting brighter.

With these two chapters working together, do we already have some support for this book's first main claim, that the religion project is undeveloped and immature? I think we do. Even if we humans had put in a stellar effort, religiously, in the time we've had, now in the past, the religion project's big ambitions might still mean that we're going to fall down and get up lots of times for who knows how long before we seriously improve.

But having brought up the past, it comes to mind that we really should take a closer look at it. Has our performance on religion so far *been* stellar?

4

A Poor Record

The religion project's ambitions are huge. Check. A lot of experiencing and growing over a great deal of time could be required to achieve them. Check. So, humans have given a lot of *care* to this enterprise in the time we've had, and great *seriousness*, *rigor*, and *diligence* in religious intellectual investigation have become a conspicuous part of the human religious record, right? Uh, well ... no. We can't put a check mark there. The present chapter explores why.

In investigation, as elsewhere, religion's own record simply leaves much to be desired. Imagine a paragraph densely packed with all of the complaints about religion that have been generated, say, just over the past decade. It would probably explode before being fully written. Now take out everything in the paragraph that's not true. It would probably still explode! It's just the case that there are innumerable bad things, and things contrary to its own ambitions, that religion must own. And these include investigative failings.

But the failures here are not religion's alone. Nonbelievers rightly come in for criticism too. Indeed, the failure to investigate religious matters properly – to put ourselves in a position to achieve knowledge about transcendent things if there is any to be had, and thus potentially release all the other changes religion seeks – is really a human failure, which we all must own.

Of course it should be noted at this point that we know very little of the details of religion in the first 44,000 years or so of its presumed 50,000-year history. And that's a considerable liability. Maybe the Cro-Magnons, our early modern forebears, had something really big and important going on religiously. But there is no evidence of this. And most of the biggest, and most intellectually stimulating, changes in the history of religion clearly have occurred alongside, and in interaction with, other significant cultural changes of the past few thousand years. So it won't be surprising that I concentrate in this chapter on our intellectual record in relation to religions still alive in the present. Mind you, this approach shouldn't be viewed as simply the product of our historical ignorance. Thinking about whether we should regard the religion project as immature means thinking about where it has been brought to by this point, and of course living religions have had a lot to do with getting us where we are. Likewise, it means thinking about how we could and perhaps should move forward from where we've arrived in the present, and this again is something we can get a better handle on only by learning about the record of religion as we see it today.

I've suggested that I'll be concentrating on our intellectual record. This isn't just because I'm a philosopher and naturally biased this way, but because positive intellectual change is such a big and critical part of the change religion promises to deliver – which in turn means that our intellectual diminishments can be used to argue that religion is immature. However, my approach in this chapter is such that many other aspects of our poor record in relation to religion will become visible for anyone who cares to see them. It's a much-neglected fact that aspects of ourselves and of our relations with others that may not directly involve thinking can nonetheless affect how well we think. In the case of religion, we have to take note, in particular, of certain facts about the moral, psychological, and social aspects of the human condition. We as humans are poorly developed in all of these areas, in ways that bear the marks of past beliefs. As a result, the investigative spirit has, in matters of religion, often been choked out by other attitudes actively militating against improvements in religious understanding.

Brace yourself, as we take a closer look at these often nasty underlying factors and their intellectual consequences.

MORAL FACTORS

I begin with the moral domain, where, among many other things, we find self-importance, greed, dogmatism, hostility, rivalry – and loyalty. These items are related in a variety of ways, as we'll soon see.

Self-importance heads the list. Deeply impressed with ourselves, as we saw already in Chapter 2, and inclined to overestimate our abilities and the magnitude of what we or people of our own time have done, we often can't clearly see how true understanding may still elude us. And so we're not motivated to seek it further. Religious investigation ends swiftly. But, you say, surely such self-importance operates as much in science as in religion, and yet science has been able to develop. That, however, is because science features self-correcting mechanisms (involving the verdict of nature and of critical peers) for which no clear counterpart exists in religion. And while no doubt our self-important tendency operates in other areas too, it's easy to see how it might be even more active religiously than otherwise, given the unrivaled significance and prestige that must naturally come with the discovery of transcendent truths.

Religious people themselves – for example, the seventeenth-century French polymath Blaise Pascal, in his *Pensées* – have often emphasized the role that a prideful self-importance can play in religious matters. But, naturally enough, they've been inclined to concentrate on its effects in nonbelievers. Nonbelief is often said to have its source in pride. Nonbelievers, so it is said, find the content of religious belief just too much of a challenge to their autonomy. Surrendering in humility to the divine requires a degree of self-forgetfulness that many nonbelievers simply can't muster. Hence they dodge the careful attention to things religious that, were they to manifest it, might allow the truth about religion to be revealed to them.

No doubt there are some people like this in the nonbelieving camp. But it's important to go beyond this observation and in all impartiality take note of how a parallel point applies to religious belief: Surrendering the notion that one is the special object of divine love or a special instrument of divine will – more generally, that one's life is intimately bound up with something of transcendent significance – requires a degree of self-forgetfulness and humility that many a religious believer would find it difficult to muster. Thus self-importance is at work in both believers and nonbelievers, in ways that contribute to keeping humans in a relatively primitive intellectual state where religion is concerned.

The second moral factor in our list is *greed*. Our thirst for knowledge, ironically, can be an obstacle to its attainment. In the intellectual realm, as notoriously in other areas, humans lack patience and want immediate gratification. We don't suffer ignorance gladly, and this even when its short-term costs ought to be accepted for the sake of long-term intellectual, and perhaps spiritual, good. The great twentieth-century philosopher Ludwig Wittgenstein once said that in the philosophy race, it's the one who gets to the finish line *last* who wins, but most philosophers don't seem to think much of such sentiments. Maybe this helps to explain all the ill-conceived metaphysical and religious systems with which history is littered. Instead of seeing themselves as contributing to a perhaps ages-long cooperative endeavor, humans feel that the truth – the final truth! – must somehow be capable of being embraced in their own lifetime. We're all vulnerable in this area, even cautious skeptics, who may be tempted grandiosely to argue that nothing at all can be known. As we saw in Chapter 2, we want to figure out all the important things now, without waiting for the future. And this greed makes its own contribution to neglect of deep religious investigation by leading to over-hastily formed beliefs.

Intellectual greed, together with self-importance (which of course will make one think that what one is greedy for can be achieved), represents one way in which a certain quite well-known tendency which we might delicately describe as 'the tendency to insist that one is right with insensitivity to the possibility of error' can be generated. This familiar phenomenon, however generated, is more bluntly called *dogmatism*. Like the states of mind and character already mentioned, this new item is an intellectual and moral vice, which is why its operation in human history is a moral factor. Dogmatism commonly is involved in a fierce resistance to what others believe on the same subject. When this is one-sided we get the next item from my list, intellectual *hostility*. When instead it's multi-sided and mutual, we have yet another item; we can call it intellectual *rivalry*. Here attention comes to be given to zealously protecting what one believes or defeating the beliefs of others. Since these dispositions and activities are, to a greater or lesser degree, bound up with tendencies toward misrepresentation, ridicule, bitterness, jealousy, possessiveness, or unwarranted resentfulness or indignation, I view them as vices also.

Now, it's pretty obvious that religious and irreligious dogmatism, hostility, and rivalry are well represented in human history. In the religious realm, as we know, much more is at stake than elsewhere, both intellectually and (as we'll see more fully a bit later on) emotionally and socially. So the struggles back and forth have been even more protracted and intense here than elsewhere, with individuals and groups for long periods engaged in combating opposed views, and rivals locked in rancorous disputes, and virtually everyone expending huge amounts of energy to defend their own view against what are seen as encroaching competitors.

This goes on all the time even today at the everyday level – think, for example, of what 'life as usual' involves in many parts of the Middle East, India, and Pakistan, and in both liberal- and conservative-dominated parts of the United States. But it has also appeared in more 'scholarly' disputes. Think, for example, of the conflicts among Christian scholars through much of Christian history over the meanings of Trinity and Incarnation, about baptism, papal authority and scripture, and concerning the Eucharist and ecclesiastical structure. And the history of discussion among and between Jewish, Islamic, Buddhist, and other religious scholars features struggles of a similar nature. On the irreligious side, hot denunciations of religion sponsored by Marxism or scientism and similar ideologies are almost as well known.

Conflicts like this have dominated religious history and the history of religious discussion, and it has to be said that, intellectually speaking, they have often been quite useless. They almost always generate more heat than light, and are more often ended by changes in other parts of the culture or society involved – perhaps an emperor comes to power or a pope dies or democracy flourishes – than by the discovery of an intellectual solution that helps people deal effectively with the disputed matters. Nourished by the vices mentioned above, such conflicts have indeed resulted in a phenomenal amount of wasted time in human intellectual history. Where a disinterested concern for the truth might have led to an enlarging of the terms of debate – with thinkers attempting to harmonize apparently conflicting insights or to find more generous perspectives that rendered the conflict irrelevant or to identify problem areas where progress could more easily be made – and also to the development of more precise tools for conducting it productively, humans have instead so very often indulged their peculiar penchant for fruitless controversy. This has clouded the issues instead of illuminating them, and thus contributed to humanity's poor record of religious investigation.

Now I've focused rather sharply and, it may seem, one-sidedly on human traits and activities of the past affecting our ability to achieve religious understanding that are ultimately rooted in self-centeredness or egoistic concern. Surely, someone will say, more attractive traits can also be detected in both religion and irreligion! Yes, indeed. I agree. But, moving on to the last item on our list of moral factors, what will become apparent is that even when we turn our minds from vice to what's commonly viewed as virtue we bump into something that may quite significantly have held us back in religious discussions of the past.

What I have in mind here is *loyalty*. The impact of religious loyalty commonly goes unnoticed. So I want to draw attention to it. First, though, let's remind ourselves that everything else I've said so far in this book underlines the need to engage in at least as searching and diverse forms of inquiry where religious questions are concerned as in science. Straining ourselves to the utmost, growing in every way possible, exploring with imaginative energy and intellectual rigor might very well be prerequisites for discovering truths about religion. And it's here that loyalty becomes especially relevant.

Remember that the reality religious believers take themselves to be in contact with is thought by them to be transcendent, maybe even ultimate, in value, both inherently and in terms of the benefit it represents. Their concern with this reality is a very deep one. Because religious belief is all wrapped up with this concern, it tends to go hand in hand with a rather fierce loyalty. Nothing less than complete devotion is appropriate where such a reality is involved. The development of the believer's moral character has therefore typically been one involving a rather generous emphasis on this trait of loyalty – notice here how common in religion are praise of faithfulness and commitment, and also censures of apathy and betrayal. And a quite natural extension of this loyalty is of course to religious belief itself. How, for example, can you remain loyal to God if you allow yourself to be seduced by objections to the belief that there *is* a God? My phrasing here is deliberate: a believer often will see arguments against her belief as a challenge to moral virtue. (Hence the common and pejorative expression 'giving in to doubt.') But what this means is that, having once formed a belief this way or that on ultimate things, the religious person is unlikely to be stirred from her position. She may think of herself as loyal to the truth, but the important thing is that she also thinks she has *found* it in her present belief. And it is her response to this that sets in motion a process making it ever more difficult to view objections to her belief, or different and conflicting conceptions of the transcendent, as serious candidates for truth. So just when she should be sitting up and taking notice of how the facts may be different from what she thought, she is likely to become more deeply invested in her belief instead. Dealing with issues that might, of all issues, be the most difficult to resolve, which therefore deserve special care and open-mindedness, she is likely rather to become stubborn and intransigent, because of well-intentioned but misplaced loyalty.

It's important to see how misplaced this loyalty is. Our fundamental loyalty in intellectual matters, here as elsewhere, should be to the truth, *whatever* that may be, and to all who seek it. Instead, many religious believers are stalled, in large part due to loyalty, right where they first thought of themselves as coming in contact with the truth about religion. When they notice that others disagree, they tend not to think of this as an opportunity for dialogue and growth toward deeper understanding, but rather feel impelled to insist on fundamental error in the opposing views. Quite independently of careful investigation, they consider much of the specific behavior and emotional life of those others to be wrongheaded, grounded in an inaccurate conception of the way things are. Such a loyal commitment to not being budged from a certain way of viewing the world, it has to be said, has done – and is doing – a great deal to prevent proper investigation of religious matters.

It's interesting and important to note that among the effects of the religious loyalty I've described is a diminished sense of the importance of religious matters among intellectuals generally. Many of those who deny or doubt that there is truth in religion have an impoverished sense of what religion is and may be, obviously deeply affected in many cases by the limitations of the actual forms of religion with which they've come in contact. There's a tendency, for example, to infer from the fact that many actual religious persons are fiercely loyal to their belief and unwilling to submit it to serious scrutiny, that religion must by its very nature be irrational, and that any commitment to creative and critical inquiry should therefore include a rejection of religion.

This is a poor inference, itself badly in need of critical scrutiny; as we'll see later, such loyalty – and even such belief – is not in fact an essential part of religiousness. But the effect is still such as to make many who might otherwise be interested in religion suspicious of it instead, and unconcerned about religious inquiry. And thus the dismissal and rejection of religion, so common among today's intellectuals, can be prevented from being any more reliably grounded than the loyal embrace of belief on the part of the religious which has caused it. More to the present point, because of these facts nonreligious people have commonly not been motivated to dig deep in their investigations of religion, and so have done no more than religious people to contribute to the advanced state that may well be needed for the deepest insights about religious matters to be achieved.

PSYCHOLOGICAL FACTORS

I've made a lot of moral points in support of the idea that religious intellectual development among humans isn't very far advanced. But, as you will have guessed, these are in many ways intertwined with psychological notions. I've already indicated this, at least implicitly, by speaking of people as *fiercely* loyal or *zealously* self-protective or *uncomfortable* with ignorance. But now let's develop the connection between psychology and beliefs about religious matters a little further.

The most obviously relevant psychological phenomenon is *emotion*. Our often unruly emotions may, as is often remarked, be a large part of what makes us human. Certainly, a complete story of the rise and many falls of our race could hardly be told without a bulky chapter devoted to them. And I don't mean to suggest that their influence is all bad. Many of the glories of human life would be quite impossible without our power of emotional response. It's also hard to imagine how a fully appropriate response to a transcendent religious reality could be completely bereft of emotion. But there are human emotions – think, for example, of jealousy and envy – that are just regrettable and can cause enormous trouble and grief; there are others which, while perhaps admirable in themselves, or at least sometimes appropriate, can become devastatingly powerful or connected to inappropriate or unworthy objects – think only of anger or love.

Such emotional states can also hold us back where religious intellectual development is concerned. This we know because they've obviously done so! It's evident that history is full of cases where individuals and groups become psychologically attached to religious or to anti-religious beliefs, by which I mean that a lot of pleasant emotion – including emotions that go with loyalty and self-importance, but sometimes also loving, trusting, grateful, joyful emotions – comes to be bound up with having those beliefs, and a psychological need or desire to keep them is (consciously or unconsciously) active. Gripped by such a condition, humans have often been far more reluctant to let go of their beliefs than is compatible with persistence in religious inquiry. Attached to this belief instead of that, they have frequently allowed themselves to become 'blinkered,' no longer open to any great diversity of experience and imagination.

Now it's true that many beliefs just come and go in the flow of life, as new information is acquired, or old information discredited. But it is equally true that others are, in their content, closer to the center of what matters to us, what we value or identify with. And such beliefs, because of the very nature of believing, which seems to put one intimately in touch with reality, will have a tighter hold on one. In such cases your belief together with your value judgment unleashes much positive emotion that would otherwise have been held in check, and the thoughts and words and actions which bear the mark of your belief will give that emotion even more room to grow. That emotion will carve a veritable channel through your psyche, you will become used to having it and what it is connected to in your life and more and more resistant to losing it or losing what permitted it to flow in the first place, namely *your belief*.

Think of what happens when somebody moves from wishing that they might win the lottery to actually believing that they've done so. All sorts of emotions are now released – there is no reason to prevent them if this has really happened – and a flurry of thoughts about what one will do with the money, words (screams!) to others about this wonderful experience, and actions of various kinds premised on this having really taken place naturally soon follow, and themselves find an important place in one's experience through memory. Now suppose that evidence is produced to show that the person who believes she has won the lottery really didn't win. What's the effect likely to be? Of course, the evidence might here be undeniable and one may sooner or later have to give in. But if it were possible to question it, to resist it, and to hang on to that belief a little bit longer, don't you think you might be successfully tempted to do so?

Now apply this to religious belief. The religious believer repeatedly experiences as really the case a state of affairs involving a transcendent reality and transcendent value, in which she is privileged to be able to participate; her thoughts and words and deeds, interconnected in complex ways, will bear the mark of this experience. Clearly such a belief must be quite close to the center of what matters to her, and thus (given what we've already seen) it may be expected to be a belief to which she is rather deeply attached. If we add that the need to retain a religious belief can be fairly easily accommodated, because where transcendent matters are concerned evidence is more easily manipulated than in cases like that of the lottery, it will become obvious how the investigation of religious matters is likely to suffer due to psychological factors clearly operative among us.

Analogous points apply to religious nonbelief, which often takes the form of irreligious *belief* – the belief that all religious claims are false. Here too psychological attachment is possible. The nonbeliever may come to positively evaluate anti-religious symbols, goals, practices, policies, people, etc. – things whose value is bound up with there being no transcendent divine reality – and come to experience approving, trusting, loyal emotions toward them. Such a state has often been realized in human history, especially recently: think here of the attitudes of some Marxists, Freudians, evolutionary naturalists, and others of a similar orientation, who are opposed to religion in general, favoring goals and policies that might allow us to move beyond it. And where such an evaluative orientation is present, an attachment to irreligious belief may be deepened. But as we all know, the more attached one becomes to one's beliefs, the more difficult it is to remain open to their falsity, and to engage in investigations that might show them to be false. Of course, here as elsewhere, humans – whether religious believers or nonbelievers – have not typically shown themselves to be especially adept at doing what is difficult, and as a result, religious investigation has often been neglected.

A last and perhaps deeper point about our emotions is that we still have so much to learn about them, and about the larger psychological world of which they are a part. Obviously, we are affected by both outer and inner realities. The possibility of extending and refining consciousness of both is critical to our development. And yet the inner world remains poorly understood. We're still largely a mystery to ourselves – as is often observed, psychology is still a young science, and startling discoveries about who we are in the inner depths of our being may well lie ahead of us. In part, this is because of the frequent dependence of psychological insight on insight in other areas, such as neurology, the study of the brain, where quite obviously much remains to be discovered.

Are such immaturities linked to a similar immaturity in religious understanding? Certainly, acquaintance with recent psychology can make some of what religious people have believed about transcendent things look rather less than impressive – a god made in our own image (and reflecting some of the less desirable aspects of the human image at that), a controlling, obsessive-compulsive, jealous, and insecure being who has serious problems with disagreement and projects his own needs on others, and so turns out to be supremely unworthy of worship – a god who is evidently not God. To the extent that such conceptions have influenced us – and it is evident that they have been influential in religious history – they have held us back. And to the extent that we may expect new and more refined ideas from psychology in the future, we may also expect new and perhaps more adequate conceptions of transcendence to emerge.

SOCIAL FACTORS

Another nest of factors underlying our poor record in the area of religion is *social* in nature rather than psychological or moral. But the factors here are similar in many ways to those already discussed, as well as interwoven with them in their operation, so I'll deal with them more briefly.

A general point to begin is that with respect to our social behavior too, and again in part because of links to other slowly maturing areas of study, there is much that remains to be learned. In his book *Behave: The Biology of Humans at Our Best and Worst,* Robert M. Sapolsky makes a point of emphasizing the many new links between biology and our social behaviors that have been discovered very recently. One wonders how much more information we'll have on such matters in another hundred years, or in a thousand, and what new ideas about, say, matters related to the social ambitions of religion, discussed in Chapter 3, will be suggested by it.

Of course, much that we already know about social matters is clearly related to a poor investigative record in the religious dimension of human life, my special theme in this chapter. Religion almost always occurs in social contexts – it is typically nurtured and even shaped by the interaction of individuals in groups; children are brought up in such communities and from an early age taught to see the world in ways sanctioned by them. Here we can as well speak of Buddhist sanghas or Hindu sampradayas or of Islamic mosques or Jewish synagogues as of the many Christian churches. And before any of these, as the archaeological evidence suggests, religion was still practiced communally.

One clue as to how such social facts are relevant to our theme comes from the fact that religious communities have tended to be quite patriarchal and authoritarian in structure, much like (most of) the broader societies in which they have appeared. The result in many quarters has unfortunately been a stifling of creative imagination and critical thought, and this from a very young age. Critical creativity has commonly been replaced by reliance on the word of shaman or elder or pastor or priest or pope or king (or king who is pope, where ingenuity sufficient to bring about such a happy coincidence has been available) – with obvious negative consequences for the possibility of any real intellectual development. There has also been a tendency for the loyalty mentioned earlier to be extended, in quite an exclusivist manner, to the religious believer's community.

All of this together produces a system in which various factors inimical to creative and critical thinking interact and are mutually reinforcing – each believer's personal loyalty to the transcendent as she conceives it, her loyalty to various associated beliefs, her loyalty to other members of her community who hold the same beliefs, as well as to authorities within the community who affirm her in those beliefs. And the word of these authorities, together with whatever relevant experiences she may have on her own or with the community (all of course mediated by the same beliefs), she will generally regard as providing sufficient *justification* for these beliefs. When psychological factors are added to the mix, it's not hard to see how the result can produce and maintain a fairly conservative approach to matters religious, thereby motivating the casual rejection of religion among its detractors noted earlier – which may be precisely what the world does *not* need if the task of religious investigation is to have any chance of being carried out properly.

In recent years, however, changes have begun to occur which have had a wide influence and suggest that the conservative system can be altered. What I have in mind here are such things as the structural changes in our societies, and their ripple effects in religious communities, which have permitted and are permitting women more of a voice where a consideration of intellectual questions is concerned. We have yet to see the full development and the ultimate consequences of this loosening of the patriarchal grip on our individual and collective selves, but indications already available suggest that changes in our thinking about a range of issues, including religious ones, may be among the results. It only stands to reason that new ideas about such issues may emerge if the voices of half the race, once largely silent, come to be heard.

While such changes suggest that we are capable of more in the arena of religious investigation than some of the more disheartening facts I've been reporting might lead one to suppose, they also expose just how far we have to go. Our poor intellectual record is made all the clearer by the fact that they are only happening *now*. Social factors, it must therefore be said, have had their own generous role to play in producing what looks like a relatively primitive intellectual situation, religiously, for human beings of the twenty-first century.

ROOM FOR IMPROVEMENT

I want to conclude this chapter by upping the volume of the hopeful notes sounded a couple of paragraphs back. It's important to see that we've not been talking about facts – such as the fact that we humans are finite beings – that must persist and may potentially pose problems no matter what we do, and even when we're doing our best. By speaking of 'failings' I have meant to imply that we could and should have done better, and a natural corollary of this point is that *we could do better now*. By taking to heart such information as I've presented, developing the self-awareness required to apply it successfully, and acquiring the drive to achieve a fuller and clearer picture of the world as it pertains to religion, we could potentially remove certain aspects of the big challenges to religious success mentioned in Chapter 3, such as seemingly irresolvable religious disagreements, and move closer to clarity about whether they might ever entirely be met. Even religious believers, who think that in some sense they have been met, should want such changes, if only to be able to make their claims with more credibility. Recent and continuing liberalizing and progressive changes in Western culture of the sort mentioned in the previous section could help to smooth the way, for example by reducing hostility and increasing openness, diminishing dogmatism, and increasing critical thinking. Those who because of the influence of such liberalizing changes are leaving religion, joining the ranks of the Nones, are in fact among those who might do the most to capitalize on the room for improvement here.

It comes down to this: The record of religious investigation exposed in this chapter is poor, but there's no reason why it should get the last word.

The vast room for improvement that we see, improvement which feasibly might be made, offers something really important to the case I've been developing for religious immaturity. After Chapter 3 things might – theoretically – still have gone either way. If we'd found that religion has shown stellar behavior and *still* is way behind, developmentally, that would actually have been support for the view that it's never going to get anywhere. But as it is, we don't know what the alternative behaviors over that time might have achieved.

And Chapter 2? How does *it* connect with what we've learned from this chapter, if at all? Again, the deep-time perspective opens our imagination to new possibilities. I suggest it's at least in part as a result of not taking that perspective into account as we think about religion that when we look at religion's poor record, many of us are inclined to treat it as a reason to give up on religion rather than considering that we may be religiously immature. The deep-time perspective helps us see how it could still be early days. Indeed, the construal of our poor record as a weak or slow start fits rather neatly into such a perspective when you think about our evolutionary origins and the foibles of humanity. Now, precisely these facts about our limitations might lead one to wonder whether a 'better approach' could ever get any traction. But given everything else we already know about evolution and in particular the cultural evolution of the recent past, mentioned above, which humans are doing more and more to direct, Chapter 2 can be a good doubt-remover. With Chapter 3 it tells us forcefully that we have plenty of time to make a bad job into a better one, and that we can reasonably accept our poor record as a mandate, not a discharge.

5

Verdict: Immature, Not Doomed

In an episode of the popular television show *The Big Bang Theory*, Sheldon finds himself in traffic court. Standing before an impatient judge, he says with his customary flourish: "Like a milking stool, my case rests on three legs." Well, the case for human religious immaturity I'm making in this book also rests on three legs: the previous three chapters. We've already spent some time getting those three legs in place. In the first section of this chapter, I complete the account of how they are positioned in relation to each other, and show how this positioning enables them to hold the weight of my claim about our developmental immaturity in religious matters. But as we'll see by the time the chapter ends and the immaturity view has been further refined, it could be that the milking stool will hold a lot more weight than that without toppling.

CUMULATIVE SUPPORT

The previous three chapters are intended to work together, providing powerful cumulative support for my view that the religion project of *Homo sapiens* is developmentally immature rather than mature as many suppose. We saw something of how this goes at the end of each of those chapters. Let's now try to get a feeling for the whole.

Because of our bias in favor of the past and general insensitivity to facts about deep time, we should be open to the idea that, rooted in an old picture of time, our sense of the *scale of religious inquiry* is just off and therefore much more time than we had imagined will be needed to complete some of what we humans have started in the way of religious investigation. Even under the best of conditions, it might take a lot longer than we are inclined to think – and, more to the point, much longer than the relatively brief period we've had – to realize goals such as those of the religion project. This will already lead one reasonably to wonder whether that project could have got very far from the starting blocks.

Now, for a human activity, the religion project features truly *huge ambitions*. In particular, the ambitions of religion itself are arguably the largest you'll find in human life. This point too can all by itself lead us reasonably to question whether the religion project has got very far, since large ambitions are more difficult to achieve. But now combine this point with the first point, about deep time. What you'll notice is that what each point can do is increased by the other: The error of temporal scale seems more likely given that the development casually assumed is immense, since big ambitions generally take longer to achieve, and that the challenges associated with large ambitions still hold us back is the more plausible when we think about deep time, and so notice the immense periods of time involved in other natural processes, including those in which nature solves its own 'challenges.' The support realized by taking deep time and the religion project's ambitions together should at the least remove the easy confidence people often feel about that project's most important achievements being behind it.

But there is still the fact of the religion project's *poor record*, intellectually and otherwise, and this, so to speak, takes us over the top, generating confidence that deeply important improvements to the quality of our inquiry into transcendent things would be made if humans continued working on religious questions in the right ways. Initially, this poor record might seem to bolster the case of the irreligious – we have in garish colors the familiar picture of religion as stubbornly non-progressive or even regressive – but in fact the opposite turns out to be true. Because of human foibles we've acted in ways (one wants to say) perversely designed to make us pursue our religious ambitions badly, and in any case have simply wasted a lot of the time we've had so far in which to pursue such goals. So, going back to the beginning of this outline of my case, the religion project has been carried on in *far from* the best of conditions. As a result we are reasonably led to think that this project could hardly reach maturity before all these failures have been *corrected*, as they would be if we put in the needed efforts. Indeed, given cultural forces presently at work which could moderate what the past has seen, this might be a particularly bad time to end the religion project.

Thus the point about the religion project's poor record all by itself provides support, and a good deal of support, for the immaturity view.

But together with the previous evidence about huge ambitions and deep time, it does so even more forcefully. If the poor record is seen in the attempt to achieve *big* ambitions, then we have even more reason to think that much of great importance remains to be done; and if we find ourselves with ages of immense duration yet to come, we have more reason to think that there is temporal room for recovery and advance. Meanwhile, the evidence of our third point gives more force to the first two in turn. Wouldn't the religion project's big ambitions provide a less strong reason to think it immature (as opposed to a failure) if we knew that under the best of conditions and with the best efforts no real headway had been made over a period of 50,000 years? And wouldn't the point about deep time be diminished if there were no reason from our poor record to think that it is still early days for religion?

As this summary of my case for religious immaturity shows, each of its three parts, like each of the legs of a three-legged stool, both does its bit to provide the desired support and helps the others do theirs. Of course the total support provided by all three together is strongest of all – and more than strong enough. It is with all this in mind that I call my case for human religious immaturity a cumulative case, and also regard it as a successful cumulative case.

IMMATURITY: SHORTCOMING AND POTENTIAL

So far in the book, to avoid distracting complications, I've been working with a somewhat rough-and-ready notion of developmental immaturity. Now that my basic evidence for our religious immaturity is out in the open, and how it's meant to work is clear, it will be good to tackle some additional issues about immaturity not raised in Chapter 1. Having focused our lens and confirmed our conclusion by dealing with them, seeing what the immaturity of the religion project, delivered to us by previous chapters, really looks like, we'll also see how it provides us with a new developmental framework for dealing with religious matters. The power of this new approach to change how we evaluate a whole host of views with a bearing on religion will become apparent in the second half of the book.

To deal with the first of these additional issues, we need to make a pretty fundamental distinction. I'll expose it with two examples of immaturity talk. Notice the difference between them. In the first example one college student says of another, whose thoughtless attitudes toward money and men have just been described to her, "She's so immature!" In the second example a parent is caught off guard by how literally her nine-year-old has taken her suggestion that the economy is in the toilet, and the other parent says, "Yeah, he's still pretty immature!"

In both cases you see someone evaluating. Indeed, that's the case whenever immaturity talk is used. (Reaching maturity, after all, is a kind of success.) There's a shared feature that – as you might expect – involves saying that someone is *less than mature* in some respect, which is to say less than developed, *undeveloped*, in that respect. In the first case what we have is a lack of development with respect to money management and mate selection; in the second case it's a lack of development in relation to the uses and subtleties of language. So the two cases are together on that first evaluative feature. But they diverge immediately afterward.

In the first case another component of evaluation is added; in the second case we have only a non-evaluative and purely descriptive addition. If she's immature in the way claimed, then something is amiss in the life of the college student. We're being told both that she's lacking something, developmentally, *and that we might have expected her already to have acquired it*. But there's nothing wrong with the nine-year-old. He's just 'at that stage' and will grow out of it soon enough. By saying this we give a description – including a kind of prediction – of how things will go for him as nature takes its course. So, with respect to maturity, which both examples agree is lacking, it's 'should be' versus 'will be.' The college student should be further along but isn't; the nine-year-old will be further along and so – naturally enough – isn't now. I call this difference immaturity *as shortcoming* versus immaturity *as potential*. Both uses of immaturity language evaluate, but the first is, as we might put it, hyper-evaluative, one evaluation stacked on top of another, while the second is a hybrid of evaluation and description.

My examples here are both examples of people's immaturity. But don't get the wrong idea: other things can be immature too, in either way. Our understanding of the brain, for example, as well as the sciences that are trying to push our understanding deeper, are often explicitly or implicitly called immature in the hybrid sense. And these things are not people! People and their behaviors are usually hovering in the background when we speak of some non-human thing as immature in the hyper-evaluative sense, since most of the things we speak of in this way are made by people, and it's because *they're* immature in that sense that this product strikes us as it does. But that doesn't prevent it from being appropriate to use the word 'immature' in the hyper-evaluative way when referring to such products. Any of a number of Trump policies announced on Twitter in 2018 might provide an example. If a pundit on CNN upon reading Trump's words said of some such policy "That's so immature!" we wouldn't be surprised, and would know just what she meant.

Notice also that the two kinds of immaturity are compatible: one and the same thing can exhibit both kinds at the same time and even in the same respect. Think of a playboy who's never had to work, having inherited all his money, and who for a time lives a life of undemanding leisure, using recreational drugs, partying, and so on. In several different ways he just never grew up; you see the developmental delay that invites the hyper-evaluative characterization 'immature.' But suppose it's also true that he just now came to himself, waking up to what he is not – responsible, discriminating, thoughtful, and so on – and the desirability of getting to be all these good things. Wouldn't he be right, as he approaches a resolution to grow up, if he said of himself wonderingly in the *hybrid* sense, "I'm still immature!" Both of two things are true here at once: He should be further along in respects *a*, *b*, and *c* and he *will* be further along in those same respects, if he puts his mind to it and persists in his effort. Immaturity as shortcoming *and* immaturity as potential. This example also helps us to see that in immaturity of the second kind, it's not always a matter only of how things will go as nature takes its course. To see immaturity as potential properly we have to say "if nature takes its course or the necessary efforts, which can be made, are made." And there's one more 'if' here that's assumed to be satisfied: if the bearer of immaturity *survives*, living long enough for the developmental changes to be implemented and take effect.

All right. So now we know the difference between immaturity as short-coming and immaturity as potential, as well as the corresponding hyper-evaluative and hybrid uses of immaturity talk. What should we do with this knowledge? First let's apply it to the religion project, and then we'll see why, for us and the immaturity framework to come, it's immaturity as potential that will predominate.

Our work on religion, as suggested by everything we've seen so far, is a broad human project that of course includes people and their doings but also includes much more, and is not reducible to any person or set of persons. If the information about our poor record from Chapter 4, the third leg of my stool, is accepted, and it should be, then we can certainly say that the religion project is intellectually immature in the hyper-evaluative sense – and morally, psychologically, and socially immature in that sense, to boot. Immaturity as shortcoming, a developmental delay, is amply exemplified here. There are all kinds of ways in which we should be further along, developmentally, in matters religious. So I'd suggest we can see pretty quickly how the immaturity of the religion project in this specific hyper-evaluative sense – immaturity as shortcoming – can be established. Having acquired that particular concept of immaturity, we can plug it right in and see how the condition of our religious behavior is illuminated.

But having reached this insight, we also need to move beyond it. When developing the cultural consequences of religious immaturity later on, the most general idea we'll be working with – as already suggested by some of our discussion in previous chapters – is not immaturity as shortcoming but immaturity as potential. Initially, we can get at this idea by saying the following: *Human religious inquiry hasn't developed very far, but we can think of all kinds of things that might be done to take it further.*

Now, there is an important connection between that thought and the evident developmental shortcomings of the religion project. Having familiarized ourselves with religious immaturity in the hyper-evaluative sense, we can both diagnose religious immaturity in the other sense more easily and see what might be needed in the way of further effort to reach maturity. Think again of the playboy. When he comes to himself, it's not hard to start making a list of things he should now do to move through the stages of development separating him from maturity. What he needs to do – thanking his lucky stars that he has been given the time to do it – is write down all the things he hasn't done when he should have, which will rather often be the opposites of things he did do when he shouldn't have.

Something similar can be said about our subject: We can point to the things we haven't done in religious matters when we should have, often the opposites of things we did do when we shouldn't have. For example, many religious and also nonreligious individuals and communities have caused developmental delays and evince immaturity in the hyper-evaluative sense because, though recognizing and even lauding how big are religious goals, they have failed to:

- cultivate due religious humility
- and so give careful attention to the development of tools for conducting religious debates productively
- and with those tools give serious deliberation and effort to harmonizing apparently conflicting religious insights, or
- find more generous perspectives that render the conflict irrelevant, or

- identify intellectual problem areas where inter-religious progress can more easily be made
- and so on.

Imagine if these had been pervasive and taken-for-granted features of the human religion project from the beginning. How much more developed our religious investigation would be! A longer and much more detailed list of such things, things that might have taken our religious development much further, could be formed just by going back over Chapter 4 with a fine-toothed comb. So here we have some more of the evidence for religion-related shortcomings and developmental delays. But having seen this, we can now turn around, facing the future, and put these things on our list of ways in which we intend to develop *further*. Recognizing the problems associated with such things as loyalty and self-importance and today also recognizing the relevant facts about our biological and cultural evolutionary development that are being delivered to us by science, we can see how things might and should have gone differently and also – by the same token – how they can still do so through additional cultural evolution of the right kind.

As this point demonstrates, our religious shortcomings and so the corresponding notion of religious immaturity will do one very important job for us. But from here on I will be keeping the latter largely in this subsidiary 'supporting role' and concentrating on the other idea of immaturity as it pertains to religion. Since this other idea is the idea of immaturity as potential, one might naturally ask, potential for what? But drawing on Chapter 1, you may already have guessed that we'll be talking about the achievement of *goals* and the realization of *capacities*. When thinking about our religious potential, we can apply either a goal-oriented or a capacity-oriented criterion. And, as it happens, there is both a more and a less demanding way of thinking about maturity when applying these criteria. Let's now add some information about the issues lurking here and their relevance to our discussion of human religious (im)maturity.

ACHIEVING A FULLER CONCEPTION OF IMMATURITY AS POTENTIAL

The availability of both a goal-oriented and a capacity-oriented criterion of potential indicates that, where immaturity as potential is concerned (and from now on, that's what I'll mean by 'immaturity' unless I say otherwise), how the realization of that potential, that development, is identified may vary.

But it won't be hard to see which of those two will be doing the most work for us here. That's because we're thinking about the maturity or otherwise of the religion project, and this we've seen to be aimed at the *goal* of completing our inquiry into whether there is a triply transcendent reality and, if so, what it is like. Clearly, the goal-oriented criterion applies here. Later, we'll see how we can take the capacity criterion along for the ride, but for now let's just assume that the potential we think of ourselves as seeking to realize when we say that the religion project is immature is the potential to reach that goal.

Now, most often in the context of immaturity talk (and this regardless of which criterion of development is applied), the developed condition – realization of the mentioned potential – is regarded as *full* or *complete* development, the reaching of a definite termination point. We generally assume that such full development will in time be attained, so long as the person or enterprise (or whatever it is) survives and the required natural events occur or human efforts, which it is possible to make, are made. The immaturity of that very literal-minded nine-year-old mentioned earlier is an example. We assume that, so long as he survives and doesn't mess up his development in some big way, he'll eventually reach the much more sophisticated and subtle understanding of language we adults enjoy, which we of course suppose is as good as it gets, the end of the road. Because it's most common, let's call this the *standard* picture of the developed or mature condition. Likewise I'll call immaturity understood with the help of this assumption *standard immaturity*.

But we need to also get acquainted with a non-standard picture. (It will end up being subsidiary to standard immaturity in the same way that the hyper-evaluative notion of immaturity is subsidiary to the hybrid one, but its subsidiary role is an important one, as we'll see.) This alternative picture is possible because the notion of maturity can be understood in two different ways. In both cases we start from the same picture of where things are at right now in their undeveloped condition. But we have a different picture of where or how far we aim to go – of what the relevant mature condition would look like.

This alternative understanding doesn't look for any complete or final attainment but instead focuses on whether *relative* gains are possible. Naturally enough I call maturity regarded this way *relative maturity* – and likewise, again, for the corresponding immaturity. The question here is whether we can get significantly closer to the realization of our potential. As an example, consider Ludwig Wittgenstein, a notoriously perfectionist philosopher who was never content with what he wrote for long, and rarely finished anything. His thoughts in 1939 on, say, the philosophy of mathematics would have been regarded by Wittgenstein as immature when compared with his thoughts on the subject in 1942. The latter showed a gain in sophistication and clarity and so in understanding, even if Wittgenstein's goal of full understanding had not in 1942 been reached, by his standards or anyone else's – and indeed even if it wouldn't ever be reached. (It wouldn't. In the philosophy of mathematics, Wittgenstein, who died at the age of sixty-two, could have used more time. For some, that's being polite.) Wittgenstein's thinking on the philosophy of mathematics in 1942, he or anyone might say, was *relatively mature* and his thinking of three years before *relatively immature*.

So we have standard maturity and relative maturity. Which one you get depends on what is plugged in as your idea of the developed condition – relative progress or absolute. One lesson here is that immaturity is certainly about being undeveloped but also about being *developed*. Someone with a severe developmental disorder (think here of the undeveloped social skills of an adolescent high on the autism spectrum) is in an undeveloped condition but not likely to develop further – and for that very reason is not appropriately regarded as immature. Being undeveloped doesn't all by itself make you immature. You also have to be able to grow up. And since there are these two different ways of thinking about what growing up involves, standard and relative, we have two different ways of thinking about immaturity.

Let's now consider how these two notions can be applied to our religious case, starting with relative immaturity.

RELATIVE RELIGIOUS IMMATURITY

The idea that the religion project is relatively immature may not seem to stick its neck out very far. Relative immaturity is a matter of degree, and *some* further development toward the relevant goal in the context of religion isn't hard to imagine. Even those who've put religion quite out of mind, rejecting it altogether, could go along with that, you may be inclined to think.

But we don't have to say that just any degree will do. And if, consistently with our previous explorations, we propose that a lot of future development is possible, perhaps at all the levels encountered in Chapter 4, moral, psychological, social, and intellectual, our idea of relative religious immaturity will seem to be made of sterner stuff.

Thus a plausible idea of *relative religious immaturity* emerges if we think about (1) human religious inquiry as we've seen it so far and how unimpressive especially Chapter 4 has shown its development arc to be assuming the relevant goal, namely the completion of inquiry into the religious topics we've identified, but also about (2) how much further we humans are now able to go in our investigation toward that goal, assuming we survive and put in the right available efforts. We're not wagging our fingers when saying this; after all, it's immaturity as potential we have in mind here. But the hyper-evaluative immaturity idea (immaturity as shortcoming) does kick in just as earlier suggested, in a supporting role. When thinking about moving further we can get quite concrete and detailed just by spelling out all the things we should have done in light of that goal but didn't do in the past. We'll then be inclined to say: "It looks like we could get at least *that* much further, morally, psychologically, socially, and intellectually." We can think about all the ways in which we might rectify the shortcomings of the past, and we will note ever deeper development as we act on what we see.

Here it may already be noted that when in this way we push further toward the goal of the religion project we are in the very nature of the case also going to be stretching the corresponding investigational capacities, if they can be stretched at all. Though the idea of goal-oriented immaturity and maturity can be seen to dominate, we could also apply the capacity criterion if we wanted to. (In a moment we'll hit on a reason to do so.)

But this discussion has been concerned with *relative* immaturity. Will its standard cousin take us to the same place or a different one?

STANDARD RELIGIOUS IMMATURITY

The big difference here is this: Since we're no longer talking about relative maturity, we'd have to actually *reach* the ultimate goal of the religion project to be mature, not just make some progress toward it by cleaning up our act. Recognizing this, we may be led to some sobering questions. Can the claim of standard immaturity really be appropriate in the religious case? After all, if we declare ourselves religiously immature in this sense, we're saying that we're undeveloped now *but will be developed, and fully developed, later on*, having reached our goal of a completed inquiry, so long as we survive and do the things we can do to get there. Relative immaturity doesn't require this much, and so especially given the remedial things we know we can do, given our previous application of the hyper-evaluative notion of immaturity, it's not hard to see that we actually are immature in the relative sense. But a claim of standard immaturity is another matter. Here, modesty about present attainment is combined with a hugely upbeat and over-optimistic assessment of where we'll be at, intellectually, in the future. Or so it may seem.

It's at this point that, as promised above, we can bring in the idea of the capacity criterion (earlier distinguished from the goal-oriented one), and specifically the notion of exhausting or *fully tapping* our religious investigational capacities. For whenever the limits of our capacities, however modest, are reached, and no further development is humanly possible, one of two things has got to be true: (i) humans have determined that there is a triply transcendent reality or determined that there is no such reality, or (ii) this has not occurred. If the former, then the proper conclusion of the inquiry is that its goal has been achieved. If the latter, then it might seem that the proper conclusion is that our inquiry's goal has not been achieved. But here we need to recall the point made in Chapter 1: that one way to achieve the goal of the religion project is to determine that truths about the divine are inaccessible to human minds. And this we would now have learned, given (ii) above. After all, we'd need something *new* in the way of capacities if knowledge of a triply transcendent reality or of its nonexistence were *subsequently* to be established. Thus, one way or the other, the inquiry is completed and its goal achieved whenever our capacities for religious inquiry in the broad sense are exhausted.

This provides a solution for the apparent problem of undue optimism on the part of the standard goal-oriented approach to religious immaturity. For, when you think about it, the capacities-based approach raises no such problem. There's no serious question as to whether, if we survive and do everything we can, standard maturity as understood by *its* lights will be reached. Human capacities, whatever they may be or come to be, by whatever definition of 'human' you care to employ, have got to run up against a finite limit sometime! But then, since, as we've just seen, the goal of the religion project as we're understanding it has got to be reached when that happens, it follows that there's no problem about whether it will be reached. So long as we survive and do everything we can, it will happen. Maybe it would take a really, really long time, but it has got to happen. Thus it's clear that we can confidently say that we really are religiously immature in the standard *goal*-oriented sense. This gives the framework I plan to construct with these immaturity ideas a lot more stability than it could otherwise have.

But of course we're a long way from anything like full maturity right now. And so we need to work toward it. And how will we do that? Well, it would be pretty odd if the answer took us to some other place than the response based on Chapter 4 we made earlier, which suggests that we should fix what the hyper-evaluative notion of religious immaturity reveals as the sorry truth about us. Until we do that, we can hardly expect to do anything else of much value. Thus the ideas of standard and relative religious immaturity we've been exploring in these last two sections could be made to work together as follows. Assuming that the human religion project is immature in the standard goal-oriented sense, we recognize that, being immature, we should expect to work toward the relevant goal in stages, and it is by applying to our investigations the idea of goal-oriented *relative* immaturity in the way recommended above that we best proceed at the *present* stage.

Given the tendency to make premature judgments about religion we've turned up in the previous three chapters, any framework for investigation we now put in place had better have room for the possibility that as a species we'll be on the religious road a long time – needing to navigate various stages of development before reaching our final goal. Of course we'd like it to be otherwise. And maybe it will be. Maybe when we clean up our act we'll immediately see the truth about religion and be able to substantiate our view. But our great impatience means that we likely overestimate the chances of that. Indeed, some of the first things we'll need to do in trying to increase our investigative maturity will be to work on developing some other attitudes. By helping us to think about both standard and relative maturity in matters religious, our immaturity framework will make it easier and more natural to recognize and act on such things.

THE IMMATURITY FRAMEWORK

A 'framework' of the sort I have in mind is a set of ideas that brings structure and organization and potentially also considerable illumination to all our thinking in a certain region. Since we now understand a range of developmental immaturity ideas and the connections between them a lot better, we're in a position to outline briefly how they can provide an excellent new framework for intellectual activity that bears on the religious dimension of human life. (We can be brief because the rest of the book, by unifying everything that's said under these developmental ideas, will help to make this clear.)

I suggest that the idea of standard religious immaturity, which of course is being understood in the goal-oriented way, should be the central idea of the new framework. Because it implies that the goal of the religion project can be reached, this idea might seem questionable, but we have seen that it is safely regarded as true. Given the interesting connection to the plausibility of capacities-based immaturity that helped seal the deal, there's no problem saying this with the full confidence required for its new status. And as to giving standard immaturity priority over relative immaturity: we've noted that there's no need to decide between these two, since they can work together nicely under the aegis of the former. The idea of standard religious immaturity, applied in the present, demands that the idea of relative immaturity be brought in. And with it, in a supporting role of its own, comes the hyper-evaluative notion of immaturity as shortcoming. So all the ideas we've been looking at in this chapter fit together neatly, producing the full immaturity framework, which might be expressed compendiously as follows: *The human religion project is standardly immature, but we can, starting now, make progress toward standard maturity if we seek to increase the project's relative maturity by diminishing its immaturity in the hyper-evaluative sense.* Let's call this combined notion, which generates our framework, the *immaturity view*.

How can the immaturity view prove helpful and illuminating if we select it as our framework for thinking about religion? Here are six ways:

(1) The immaturity view immediately provides a context for understanding everything that's been going on in the previous chapters of the book, and in particular shows that common presuppositions of maturity on both sides of various religious debates are highly premature and unjustified. It provides a natural 'home' for that conclusion and for the ideas in earlier chapters – a single snapshot picture of the human religious condition in which they conspicuously appear. This picture is the bigger picture which everything said in previous chapters can be seen as hinting at.

(2) As subsequent chapters will show, the immaturity view, by giving ideas of transcendence a new lease on life, also has clear and transformative consequences for a variety of popular and influential views and subject areas whose assessments of religious matters have often misled us.

(3) The immaturity view furthermore allows us to identify some circumstances in which final rejection (or, alternatively, a

declaration of success) would be an appropriate response to religion, should we survive: such circumstances would obtain if, when we have grown beyond our present immaturity, we also achieve maturity by discovering the existence or nonexistence of a triply transcendent reality.

(4) The immaturity view also tells us, more positively, what evaluations we should be making relative to religion in the present. We should, first of all, evaluate religion and religious inquiry as immature (in the detailed sense previous sections have refined) rather than as a success or as a failure. But in this connection the immaturity view, while keeping its own focus on human potential, also makes good use of the hyper-evaluative immaturity idea, which allows us to infer the availability of a new agenda for present investigation from knowledge of the shortcomings we can fix.

(5) By thinking of religious investigation as immature, we also get some more specific leads as to what we should now be doing in the religion project. It will seem natural and appropriate, for example, to say that a preliminary focus on the methods of collaborative investigation and on acquiring the humble attitudes appropriate to immaturity would be a good thing. Also, questions about more general matters – such as the very ideas of transcendence and ultimacy – and attempts to work out new possible understandings of transcendent things may be seen to take precedence over further exploration of detailed existing religious conceptions.

(6) Finally, reflection on our immaturity might even prompt the discovery of new forms of religion – forms of religion *appropriate specifically to immaturity*, which for that reason we have overlooked.

We might think of all the time and effort that humans are putting into religion as a kind of *test* of the idea that its high ambitions can successfully be pursued by us. By accepting this immaturity framework and working within it, we are signaling our agreement that the test should go on. For how long? 100 years? 1,000? 10,000? Remember deep time. Remember all the obstacles that our finite evolved quirks have presented to the religion project, and will present to efforts of the future. Remember all the improvements that need to be made. Remembering all this, we may see the usefulness of going with a big number, *especially* now, when we need continually to be reminded of the changed perspective that will be required for religion to get anywhere at all. So I propose we try to imagine another 10,000 years, and think of the test as a 10,000-year test of the sort parenthetically mentioned in the prologue.

If the changed perspective is to take hold, we will need to make some more specific adjustments to a range of views, presently popular in our culture, which directly or indirectly bear on religion, often in negatively evaluative ways, and which reflect the unchanged perspective. The immaturity view has transformative consequences for them. The second half of the book spells out these consequences. Though we've just given ourselves 10,000 years, there's no time to waste. Let's get started.

6

A New Path for Science and Religion

In "Atheism, the computer model," a recent article in *Nautilus*, Michael Fitzgerald reports on the latest data-driven studies of how societies become supernaturalist, fall away from supernaturalism, and return to it when the going isn't good. The article concludes with the thoughts of Boston University's Wesley Wildman, who ventures the view that supernaturalism isn't likely to disappear, since people have "a basic propensity – a biological imperative – toward a desire to ascribe actions to an agent, a being, even one we cannot see." As Wildman puts it: "Every generation is born supernaturalists."

Here we have an example of work being done in *science and religion*, a field of study that since the 1960s has been exploring relations between the two areas of human life joined in its name, especially those that appear to have a bearing on religion's intellectual value. In the *Nautilus* example, the influence of thinking in the cognitive science of religion (CSR), now often treated as included in science and religion, is apparent. Many think of CSR as providing broad support for the idea that the tendency for humans to believe in gods who are agents, who *do* things, is no evolutionary accident. Your survival is aided by noticing when agents who can hurt or help are in your vicinity. And, especially in an age before science, gods would easily have been added to the list of live possibilities. If god-related mental and social behavior sticks around, perhaps because it ends up being adaptive in ways not imagined by those who first thought of gods, related propensities can be passed along evolutionarily and show up on busy modern city streets or even in the brains of sophisticated scientists.

It's not hard to see how these facts – if indeed they are facts; CSR is still a quite youthful science – could be used to try to debunk religious ideas, whose advocates often take them to have a more recent provenance. Eager to accommodate such findings within their own perspective, believers have sometimes responded by arguing that they come with the fingerprints of a personal divine reality who wants to ensure that there will be a way to be noticed. And so the science and religion discussion finds its usual grooves and carries on.

But here's another example, or potential example, of work on science and religion that might lead in a different direction. Let's start with the science. In their contribution to a book of essays published by Cambridge University Press on biocultural co-constructivism, brain scientists Thad A. Polk and J. Paul Hamilton point out that reading, writing, and arithmetic are "recent in evolutionary time," are "not shared with other species," and don't "develop without instruction," and yet there is evidence – for example, their selective impairment through brain damage – that these functions reflect distinct "anatomic modules in the human brain." This, they argue, shows that cultural evolution can result in new brain developments, and so we're not stuck with what biology has made innate. (Of course more general cognitive and neural mechanisms that *are* innate will presumably be required for such later developments, as they acknowledge.) "Apparently, the brain can reshape its modular architecture in response to the most important demands of its culture."

I don't know whether these scientific results will hold up under the pressure of future study. But suppose they do. Suppose they're at least as reliable as those of CSR. Then we might wonder – and here's the application to religion – whether in an analogous way (and no doubt aided by reading, writing, and arithmetic) new brain modules involving more subtle thinking both about *causation* and about *supernatural* causation could be built on the cruder innate base suggested by our first example of work on science and religion. Might the right cultural changes associated with religion, perhaps over much time, enable this to happen? If so, we might agree with Wildman but go further than he seems prepared to do: Supernaturalism may indeed not disappear; but instead of constantly recurring in primarily agential forms, it may after much additional cultural activity become far more sophisticated and discriminating, moving on from basic agency to other forms a transcendent reality might take, including ones as alien to *Homo sapiens* today as the facts and figures of arithmetic once were.

I'm not interested in settling this particular issue here, but I do want to draw attention to the fact that we wouldn't even see its pertinence, in science and religion, if we hadn't started to think of work on religion as a *developmental* phenomenon in something like the way being recommended in this book. New insights become possible when we do. Indeed, pretty much everything we've said in this book so far is either directly or indirectly relevant to a new understanding of the relationship between science and religion. The rest of the chapter explores how more systematically. And here and there in the rest of the book I'll be taking the opportunity to fill out the picture. As we'll see in the present chapter, when brought into the immaturity framework a number of common assumptions about science and religion unfriendly to the latter's survival and flourishing in a robust form are put out of commission, and at the same time, a quite new and positive conception of the relationship possible for those two is able to emerge. It's part of the hidden power of a developmental perspective on religion, in other words, to nudge us out of our usual ruts in science and religion and onto a new path.

MUST SCIENTIFIC CONSEQUENCES FOR RELIGION BE NEGATIVE?

The first common assumption about science and religion that must be given up if we accept a framework of developmental immaturity for the religion project is that scientific results, insofar as they have a bearing on religion at all, must have a *negative* bearing.

This assumption has grown from the frequency with which, in our past, popular religious explanations of things, usually featuring divine agency of one sort or another, have butted heads with scientific explanations. And there is plenty of potential for such conflict still today. If you think that the universe was directly created by God 6,000 years ago or that epileptic seizures are examples of demonic possession, modern science will have a bone to pick with you.

Now, there are whole industries within traditional religion devoted to dealing with such conflicts. Some traditional thinkers say that science is just wrong; others, less foolhardy, hold that the conflict is, for one reason or another, only apparent. Perhaps, for example, the scriptural passages that motivate the anti-scientific religious claim can be reinterpreted or are dispensable within a new understanding of scriptural authority. Still others, more boldly, try to turn the tables on the assumption in question, arguing that at least a general idea of personal divinity is *supported* by certain scientific results, such as those that involve the apparent 'fine-tuning' of the universe, at the time of the big bang, for the production of intelligent life. They may produce such arguments, as the British philosopher Richard Swinburne notably has done, in the context of a broader case for the view that the idea of an agent God is needed to *complete* the intellectual account science gives us – to explain those things, such as the fact that a complex physical universe exists at all, that science by its very nature must leave unexplained.

Here we are, again, in the usual grooves. That our immaturity framework takes us to a new plane is evidenced by the fact that, given the developmental approach, *even if all these religious ways of dealing with our present problem failed, there'd be no reason for defenders of religion to get worried*. Indeed, the religion project would have reason to regard such information as rather useful, since by motivating us to set aside certain religious ideas that aren't working, intellectually speaking, it could only aid the ongoing attempt to discover any true religious ideas there may be and also to improve religion in various ways by dealing with our religious shortcomings. A particular form religion might take, as it evolves through such changes, is described in Chapter 9.

That the developmental approach puts the religion project in a new and improved position vis-à-vis scientific results is also evidenced in other ways. As we'll see in Chapter 8, it allows a new defense against an anti-religious view often *built* on scientific results, namely, metaphysical naturalism. The developmental approach, furthermore, is itself nurtured or inspired by scientific ideas whose relevance to religion we might otherwise have failed to notice. I'm thinking of the notions of physical development and evolution, which, even if they receive more specific applications in science, are certainly pervasive in its precincts. And of course there is the idea of deep time and other similarly 'large' ideas in science which can inspire us to move to a macro-level perspective of things. Such a move is not resisted but rather *presupposed* by the developmental picture of the religious dimension of human life I have defended. By making it, we show how humanity's imagination in religious matters can grow to be as big as it is in science.

WOULD RELIGION BE AS DEVELOPED AS SCIENCE,
IF THERE WERE ANYTHING TO IT?

Another common assumption about science and religion that must be set aside by anyone accepting a framework of developmental immaturity for the religion project is the assumption that if religion were going to succeed in its ambitions, sketched in Chapter 3, it would have done so by now or at least be as far along as science appears to be in relation to *its* goals.

A presupposition of capacity-oriented religious maturity is here visible, and it should be clear by now that there is ample reason to resist it. Religion might be able to deliver the goods – where by 'the goods' is meant, again, what *robust, transcendently oriented* religion is after – but do so only in the future, perhaps the far future, after many remedial changes have been implemented and our capacities have been commensurately improved. Of course it might also fail to do so. But at this early stage of development we are in no position to rule out success. Religion today, as I mentioned in Chapter 1, may be at a stage of development something like science's in the Middle Ages. This is indeed what we should be inclined to say even on an assumption of eventual success, if we factor in how we appear to be much better at science than we are at religion and notice our vast immaturity-as-shortcoming in the religious domain – including even the absence of any clear sense that religion *might be* a developmental phenomenon.

The assumption at issue here has made a lot of unnecessary trouble for religion, which in relevant respects has often seemed backward, disorganized, unsophisticated by comparison with science. It hasn't helped that religion's defenders – including those many to be found in the science and religion debates – are inclined to make the same assumption! Although they do it positively instead of negatively, they too presuppose that religion is already mature. Not being in a position to contest that assumption, it has remained a thorn in their side. All of this changes, in obvious ways, when we take away the constraints that for no good reason have made us try to push and shove and squeeze the development of religion entirely into the past. Such a static view of religion today has nothing to commend it, and should itself be left in the past.

IS RELIGION CLOSED TO THE NEW, WHILE SCIENCE IS OPEN AND EXPLORATORY?

A third common assumption that may now be dispensed with is that religion of its very nature must fail to exhibit the open and exploratory attitudes of science.

This assumption, which would make a presupposition of its own maturity part of what it is *to be* religion, is tempting because much religion today is indeed just as here described. The question, however, is whether religion must be so, whether it is in its very *nature* to be so, and this question our developmental view answers resoundingly in the negative. Now, you may still be inclined to wonder about this answer. How can there be anything properly called *religion* that does not promise to answer our deepest questions with truths already discovered, and so provide an emotionally secure basis for living? Well, when we see through the immaturities that have made such (over)optimism so attractive, religion too may start to grow up. In Chapter 9 we'll get an idea of what a more mature religiousness might look like.

It's imagination, perhaps more than anything, that's in demand here. In fact, all we really need to imagine is a single addition being made to religion: curiosity. I'm thinking of a *deep* curiosity, though, not a shallow one: a curiosity fed by a love of the truth, whatever it might be, and by a recognition that, given our various limitations and immaturities, the truth of things might be far more impressive, in its furthest contours, than we have yet imagined. Such curiosity could function as a fundamental motive, making religion open and exploratory too. Under this star, religion could begin to look a lot more like science in the relevant respects.

Perhaps a story will help us imagine how this could happen. So suppose that as the twenty-first century continues to unfold, the world is ever more filled with violence, with more and more money diverted from scientific investigation to help manage various 'wars on terrorism' that are spiraling out of control. In the midst of this deepening chaos on Earth, attention to observing the skies diminishes, and – you guessed it – a large asteroid that might in better days have been noticed and perhaps averted plunges into Earth, leaving much of it in ruin.

The human costs are huge. Nearly everything is lost. But through luck and enormous effort, some few human beings and some significant traces of past culture and knowledge are enabled to survive. Over many centuries and then millennia of struggle and adaptation in the midst of greatly altered circumstances, old knowledge slowly comes to be developed in novel directions and cooperative survival skills evolve into traditions of greater intellectual flexibility and interdependence. Then a sort of 'golden age' arrives, in which, experiencing relative stability, the people of the world are able to turn their attention more fully to science and art and the pursuit of knowledge about big questions for its own sake.

In this golden age, despite a few lapses into aggressive and competitive behavior, humans from every part of the planet manage to incorporate into their activities something of the cooperative ethos created by their unique history. Despite a natural ebb and flow, they succeed in retaining the support of their broader communities in a manner that is in striking contrast to what had been the norm prior to – what is now called – the *Catastrophe*. The result is a great and indeed unprecedented flowering of intellectual life. Scientific, philosophical, and religious forms of thought come to be interwoven in creative ways, and new conceptions of transcendent and ultimate things emerge, in part through the metaphorization of key elements of new scientific ideas (which have long since eclipsed both Newton and Einstein). Institutes for the study of religion and psychology, of religion and politics, of religion and art, and of religion and philosophy, as well as many similar institutes with names you wouldn't recognize, dot the landscape in every populated region, with various levels of parent institutes and partnering institutes connecting the dots in diverse ways. And their ideas, together with the ideas of other cultural institutes and organizations, dot the *mental* landscape, so that an enormous intellectual and spiritual synergy is created.

So much for the main part of the story. I suggest two alternative endings.

(1) There follows a period of many thousands of years which, while seeing countless other changes, preserves unbroken a strand, sometimes thicker, sometimes thinner, of intense communitarian intellectual inquiry. It deeply penetrates the various possible construals of transcendent things that arose from the aforementioned synergy and one by one they are shown to be in some deep way confused or incoherent, or else proven to correspond to nothing in reality. The world sees another thousand years of work in which, despite much brilliant effort, no new religious ideas are discovered and a great deal of 'experimental religion' yields ever diminishing returns. With scholars and non-scholars alike concluding that nothing of distinctive or enduring value is to be found in religious practice, and science meanwhile going from strength to strength, religious thinking gradually dissolves into a holistic morality fostered in the context of a tentative metaphysical naturalism, which the human beings of this advanced age take with them into their future.

(2) There follows a period of many thousands of years which, while seeing countless other changes, preserves unbroken a strand, sometimes thicker, sometimes thinner, of intense and deeply penetrating communitarian intellectual inquiry. Science goes from strength to strength, but meanwhile there also grows from this

strand of communitarian inquiry a consensus, among people of the Earth, concerning the value of a single religious idea, which scholars and non-scholars alike declare to be an idea of unparalleled beauty and richness. It is an idea which gives a finer and fuller texture to the notion of transcendence than any previously encountered, while allowing indefinite extension and application in theory, practice, and both individual and communal experience. Moreover it proves quite compatible with all that has been learned from science. Another thousand years pass in which, despite much concerted effort, no defects are discovered in The Idea and sophisticated arguments provide untarnished evidence that it is realized. With much 'experimental religion' confirming its multi-dimensional potency in practice, life on Earth, influenced by these results, has come to be transformed in innumerable positive ways, and – needless to say – the human beings of this advanced age take both The Idea and science with them into their future.

So ... choose your ending. Whichever ending it is, I suggest, you'll have a story that *could be true* in which religion has developed to the point where it is as open and exploratory and exhibits as much curiosity as science. It follows that the assumption we are critiquing, which says that religion's nature precludes this, is false.

WILL RELIGION BE SUPERSEDED BY SCIENCE?

Back in Chapter 1, I noted how a number of thinkers have held that it's religion's fate to give way before other cultural forces and be superseded by science. People will eventually live entirely within the latter's constraints, guided and perhaps inspired by its discoveries. Or so many have supposed. Once – as, for example, when Comte was saying this sort of thing in the nineteenth century – the idea was that there is a kind of law of history *determining* that progress will move in this direction. 'Laws of history' haven't been very popular in our own time, however. They don't seem very scientific! But this hasn't prevented various other ideas and feelings from causing people today to speak similarly. Those who love science and feel an animus toward religion are especially likely to do so, though sometimes the tone is one of hopeful aspiration more than confident prediction.

By now there are other reasons to doubt this assumption about how religion and science are related, our fourth. Religion is proving more durable than it was thought to be by those pushing a 'secularization hypothesis' only a few decades ago. No doubt the people involved in the *Nautilus* study mentioned at the beginning of this chapter would have an idea or two about why that is. But the developmental view I have presented provides its own quite unique basis for doubt about the present assumption. If people pick up on the developmental immaturity of the religion project, and this awareness spreads through the culture, religion might live on for thousands of years. It might take new and improved forms instead of being superseded by science. There is all the more reason to imagine things going this way if we imagine its *harmony* with science, as we may if, for example, we contemplate how curiosity could become a religious motive – as we did in the last section.

Someone may at this point be inclined to caution that imagining religion a certain way is rather different from it ever getting to be that way. Indeed it is. But when we're talking about cultural phenomena, we're talking about things that *often* get the way they are precisely because people imagine something new and this gets the ball rolling. Imagination is a powerful force. It would be nice to see more of it in the field of science and religion. The developmental view of this book allows us to expand the range of relational possibilities considered in that field. Instead of working within artificial constraints set by some combination of the assumptions I'm dissecting, or by things – such as a maturity presupposition for religion – that allow artificial constraints to flourish, we can get clear about the religion project's immaturity and all the new results made possible by it. Some of them, including a new way of being religious and a new sort of religious humanism, will be discussed later in the book.

OF THESE TWO, SCIENCE AND RELIGION, IS ONLY SCIENCE REALLY A FORM OF *INQUIRY*?

There's a lot hidden in our fifth assumption – the idea that religion and science are fundamentally different because the latter is a form of inquiry while the former decidedly is not. We can think of it under at least two different interpretations. According to one, this assumption, just like the others so far, takes religion to be a *fact-oriented* enterprise and dismisses its power in that regard. In other words, it's basically an insult. Under the other interpretation we can see this assumption as representing an attempt, on the part of religion's defenders, to insulate it from scientific critique by protesting that religion is something *other* than a fact-oriented enterprise. The standards of inquiry into facts, on this second interpretation, are just misapplied when brought against religion. When this happens, religion's nature has been misunderstood.

So both an *irreligious* and a *religious* interpretation are possible here. I've already addressed the main ideas of the latter in the third section of Chapter 1, and I'll be looking at a more specific version of it in the next section of this chapter. So let's set it aside for now. The former, irreligious interpretation itself can be taken in a couple of different ways. One says that religion has got nothing seriously worth inquiring *about*, and we should take its fact-oriented talk of transcendent realities as otherwise motivated – by the desire for existential security, perhaps. The other holds that religion by its very nature must constantly get distracted by the non-inquiry-related features of religiousness – by the comfort afforded by belief amid experiences of worship, for example – in such a way that its inquiry, which could in principle be more interesting, ends up being half-hearted or insincere instead and also ineffectual. This last idea I think may be set aside too, because it was dealt with implicitly a couple of sections back, when we told our story about a possible future for the religion project. Here, then, I'll focus on the other notion, that religion, unlike science, has got nothing seriously worth inquiring about.

First notice that by forming its view in terms of a religion *project*, of which the actual practice of religion is a part, and by taking us to what I've called the macro level, the developmental approach of this book is in effect calling for a *reappraisal* of the idea that religion has got nothing seriously worth inquiring about. When we see how the sub-standard quality of our religious inquiry so far can be understood, within this frame of reference, as reflecting developmental immaturity, we make even more room for the assessment that there is something worth inquiring about, all right, and we've just been doing it badly.

And this assessment seems correct. The religious questions about transcendence, and about whether nature exhausts reality, are just fascinating big questions. Some people behave as though there's something intrinsically wrong with asking such questions. Perhaps the most charitable interpretation one can place on such behavior is to say that it's an overreaction to how most people in the history of religion have arrived at – or hung on to – their religious ideas, or to the unworthy childishness of some of those ideas. But when we think within the developmental framework I've tried to hammer into place, we're less likely to fixate on these features of past religiousness. We're more likely to notice the general idea of *triple transcendence* and start thinking about this and its prospects more objectively. Might there be a reality deeper than nature that's ultimately also going to be friendlier than nature? Why isn't this something to inspire curiosity and inquiry? It would be amazing and wonderful – and this from a purely intellectual perspective – if there were such a reality, just as it would be amazing and wonderful if the fundamental facts about *nature* turned out to be quite different from what we had supposed in, say, the way envisaged by defenders of loop quantum gravity.

Once we start to think about the religion project in this way, we'll also notice how radically ambitious it is and how much we're signing on for by joining it. And that itself will motivate us to be scrupulously careful and think long term. Humans have already had a lot of trouble just trying to probe nature's depths. For an example, think of all the developments involving telescopes, which started with Galileo and have slowly led to the Hubble telescope presently poised in space, which – after many years of further laborious efforts and delays – will itself be replaced by the even more exciting and ambitious James Webb Space Telescope in a few more years' time. If there were something *beyond* nature (beyond in a metaphysical or ontological sense) it would by definition be of a different order, a different kind of reality, even if one that in some way could affect the physical world – and maybe it would be one we're not very good at detecting and understanding.

But that's right now. Immature we may be, but for intrepid explorers such immaturity only calls for strenuous efforts toward greater maturity. And such efforts we might expect to bring the religion project and science closer together, in at least a couple of ways. For from science we can learn something about the *attitudes* appropriate to serious inquiry in any area. (Of course science got them from its mother, philosophy, which honed them in the agora of Athens.) Moreover, it's natural to want to get the basic facts about nature before expecting to get very far at the religious level, since there might be clues in nature's structure and organization to how realities beyond nature are at work in it, if any are.

My points in the previous two paragraphs are not strictly needed for my denial of the view that religious inquiry isn't worth doing, but I have added them to display how we can use our developmental perspective not only to show that that alleged disconnection between religion and science isn't real, but, at the same time, to dig up some new *connections* between science and religion.

IS SCIENCE ABOUT FACTS, AND RELIGION ABOUT VALUES?

A couple of decades ago, Stephen Jay Gould, the well-known Harvard paleontologist and evolutionary biologist and beloved science writer, came out with a book defending the idea that science and religion are just on different tracks and never the twain shall meet. "Non-Overlapping Magisteria," he called them. Science deals in facts, and religion in value and meaning. One can also imagine a normative version of this view, according to which that's how things *should* be even if they aren't that way right now. Both interpretations have faced stiff opposition, though Gould's view continues to have its defenders. We noted in the last section and in Chapter 1 that some have thought it's a mistake to view religion as being about inquiry. Here we see one way in which this view can be filled out, by interpreting inquiry factually and providing religion with a different job.

The developmental approach that, in this book, has led to the immaturity view is going to be opposed to Gould's view, too. It provides its own powerful *reason* for taking a different view of things. This obviously is that we haven't yet even come close to giving the notion that religion might expose important facts – including value-involving facts – a fair shake. Gould, like pretty much everyone else, was influenced by the static view that what you see is what you'll get: that what was and is now is also what forever shall be in the religious domain. If that's your view, then it makes sense to take religious ideas, which seem to be about transcendent facts, and, say, metaphorize them for moral and other value-related purposes, instead of looking for better, more factually successful religious ideas. But on a proper developmental view, such an approach will seem at best premature. Even on this view, you might metaphorize Christian or Islamic or Buddhist or some other conventional set of detailed religious ideas if you regard them as literally false, and can get some benefit from them that way. But you'll also remain open to the *literal* truth of *other* religious claims, working to expand efforts that push beyond the conventional and open up religious frontiers. It's still early days for the religion project, and who knows what it may turn up in the way of new and profound facts?

A NEW AND POSITIVE RELATIONSHIP BETWEEN
RELIGION AND SCIENCE

One of the latest, most up-to-date, additions to the science and religion debate is a book by the philosophers Michael Peterson and Michael Ruse called *Science, Evolution, and Religion: A Debate about Atheism and Theism*. Published by Oxford University Press, the book is advertised as being, among other things, "comprehensive." As its subtitle suggests, however, this is either false or a sad commentary on the condition of the science and religion field! Peterson and Ruse are both somewhat one-sidedly influenced by Christianity in religious matters, and treat theism's idea of an agential personal divine as a boundary concept for religion. This is how they see things, even though in other forms of religion claiming millions of adherents in the world today, the agential notion of divinity is left behind. Consider, for example, Theravada Buddhism and the Advaita Vedanta stream of thought and practice in Hinduism. Moreover, as we saw at the beginning of this chapter, when we mentioned CSR, you need only poke around a bit in *science*, reflecting on what you find, to see how *agential* concepts of triple transcendence might represent but the bare beginning of the human religion project. The science and religion field needs to do better.

The developmental approach of this book could help it do so. Only by thinking of ourselves as engaged in a project that embraces everything religious in human life so far (not just theism and Christianity) and also pushes to understand *new* conceptions of transcendence could our work in the subject ever be truly comprehensive. Only then could it be true to the investigative impulses of science, which, as we've seen, could become religion's too – and will need to become religion's too if the project is to overcome its past shortcomings.

Here we can already get a glimpse of the more positive relationship between robust religion and science that I've been advertising. It will serve to bring it clearly into view if we work with a typology made famous by Ian Barbour, a science and religion pioneer. Barbour speaks of Conflict, Independence, Dialogue, and Integration as ways of modeling the relationship between science and religion. There are alternative typologies, and Barbour has tinkered with his own. But for my purposes these things won't matter.

Let's start here by noticing how a somewhat naïve assumption has been affecting the discussion of such typologies in the short history of work on science and religion. This is that science and religion are *at about the same stage of development, equally mature.* We don't wonder whether the thinking about the world of a seven-year-old boy and his adult brother, a college graduate, can be brought into a useful dialogue or be integrated, thus yielding a larger understanding. We say: "Let's wait for the seven-year-old to grow up!" Nor do we infer from any conflict between their thoughts that there's no hope for the seven-year-old or that the brother must be mistaken, as do those, in the analogue, who side with religion against science or with science against religion. Another way to notice the mistake here is by observing how we behave, when thinking of such models as Dialogue or Integration, as though it has to be now or never. This we wouldn't do if our thoughts had ever tasted the idea of the religion project's developmental immaturity.

When we do come into contact with that idea, we'll reject the naïve assumption. But it doesn't follow that we have to reject the typologies. For perhaps they can be understood developmentally. Barbour would never have said that all four models apply, for they certainly look mutually incompatible when we're thinking only of the present and assuming joint maturity – when it's now or never. But on a *developmental* view the application of all four becomes logically possible, for different models may apply at different times. And an overall picture, one displaying how religion and science can get along – over time and also at our time – is achieved once this is taken into account.

We could put it this way. Sure, Conflict manifestly applies to the relationship between modern science and at least the intellectual side of most past forms of religion, including a goodly number that have survived into the present. But we've seen – and will see more fully later in the book – how the human religion project could mature as new forms of robust religion emerge that provoke no conflict with science, because they are too modest to make confident truth claims or to seek to mingle their ideas with science's in the latter's intellectual playing field. In this way we might reach Independence, a kind of compartmentalization after conflict, even if it is in part scientific results such as those involving evolution and deep time that give a boost to any attempt to get religion to this point. Notice that this isn't the kind of independence or compartmentalization that Gould was thinking about with his Non-Overlapping Magisteria. (For one thing, an immature area of human life can't very well function with the authority required for a magisterium!) What I mean is a kind of time-out or space for further religious evolution to occur. Now, it's conceivable that at another, later stage of cultural (and perhaps biological) human evolution, we will have developed enough religious maturity and insight to make some form of religious belief intellectually credible and illuminating, perhaps even to the point that one of the positive, grown-up sorts of relationship signaled by Dialogue and Integration is established with a more fully evolved science. But this can be no more than eschatological aspiration for the religious today, and hardly need enter their thinking in any serious way.

The overall picture, just like any full and accurate picture of science, is one of a *human project* that changes and grows over time. *Homo sapiens* can have more than one such project, and even if science is in some ways more fully developed, there's nothing in science to say that the religion project should not be pursued, when the latter is understood as we've understood it here. As for how the two are related in the present, the immaturity view allows us to leave the conflict stage behind and enter the stage I've called compartmentalization after conflict. This is how things would stand now, in the present, if we followed its advice. We don't have to rest content with old proclivities and think about the relations of science and religion on the assumption that those proclivities must persist, as though we were already religiously mature. Religion can develop. And if it develops as it should, a kind of compartmentalization after conflict, which allows time for the religion project to deal with some of its shortcomings, will be the result.

Of course these categories are only rough indicators. It is hard for any of them to hold so rich and fluid a phenomenon as religion or science or both together. We might note, for example, that at our present stage, as envisaged by the immaturity view, religion could still be of some help to science, by supporting its results in the public domain, or even by advocating the use of scientific results to solve urgent human problems. (Chapter 10 has some related discussion.) So the notions of 'compartmentalization' and of 'independence' should be taken somewhat loosely. Whatever you call it, it's clear that at the present stage, and indeed at any future stage, there could be perfect harmony between religion and science, much as there can be perfect harmony between the seven-year-old boy and his elder brother. As the title I've given to this present section suggests, the developmental approach that brings this relationship into view is certainly positive – and it is also new.

7

The New Agnosticism

Since 2006, a band of merry men, the new atheists, has been rampaging across the science-and-religion landscape. Often these men seem angry, but really, and none too secretly, they enjoy sticking it to religion. Their approach – too impatient and confident to abide much reasoning, at least absent a healthy dollop of sarcasm – is not calculated to win the affection of serious thinkers. But serious thought is not what the new atheism is really about; serious thought is altogether *too* serious and also too timid for many new atheists. As to timidity, this tends to be what the new atheists suspect of anyone who would rather be called 'agnostic.' A term devised to describe himself by Thomas Huxley – Darwin's bulldog, not exactly a timid type – 'agnostic' reeks to many of faltering indecision. Darwin too claimed it. Everyone who's read about his life can agree that *he was* a bit timid, as well as academic and serious, though for some reason this is rarely the emphasis when Darwin's theory of evolution by natural selection is used by new atheists to attack old beliefs.

For the new atheist, it's God or Science (and guess who wins). The old agnostic, who thinks atheism goes too far, is unsure about a personal God, thinking there might be one and also might not be. Just to keep the record straight, let me say at this point that I am not an agnostic in *this* sense. I have written books defending the view that there is no God. If it were God or Science, I too would go with Science, but things at our immature stage of development aren't as neat and tidy as that. What we see in these disputes is just one pocket of the world's cultural life, actual and potential. In this pocket God and Science tend to be the only live options. But out in the light where the world's cultural life, actual and potential, can breathe and have its being and stride free, things are a good deal more rich and interesting than that.

AGNOSTICISM AND IMMATURITY

As you might expect, I would like you to interpret that last sentence in terms of the earlier arguments of this book. If we accept that the religion project is developmentally immature in the sense recently arrived at – and by now perhaps you'll agree that we should – and if we think this through, then we'll accept that we might so far have done no more than dip our toes in an ocean of religious possibilities; God is just one of the fish in the sea. Moreover, impatient, overconfident, and sarcastic intellectual activity on religious matters, however entertaining it may be, is not exactly designed to turn up other fish, if there should be any. It looks like just another example of immaturity-as-shortcoming. (A way of interpreting what the new atheists are up to as quite distinct from religious investigation, and so not necessarily subject to such a criticism, is however possible and mentioned later in the chapter.)

Now, it could be that even at our present stage of investigational immaturity, with so many shortcomings – especially in religion itself – to make up for, we humans can deal with certain relatively uncomplicated challenges, like assessing the intellectual merits of exclusively personal gods. Perhaps there's good reason to deny – that is, to disbelieve in – the existence of God. For now let's just assume there is and that the new atheists, without deserving much credit, are nonetheless right about that much. Even so, we might only have disturbed the first layer of transcendent possibilities. The seventeenth-century philosopher Baruch Spinoza thought that the physical and the mental were just the two modes of the divine accessible to us, out of an infinite number of modes in Nature, which he would have called the *real* God. Notice that his Nature towers over nature as understood by the new atheists, at any rate in its daring and imaginative appeal. I don't know if Spinoza was right, but the idea does provoke and prod us to determine whether we really want to know what the truth is, no matter *what* it is. I don't know either whether Spinoza would have thought that time might bring more relevant thoughts – thoughts not about the physical or the mental but about other realities – within our grasp. But this idea too should prod our hominin imaginations. As Chapter 2 and Chapter 5 together help us to imagine, not only are we investigationally immature in the religious realm, but our immaturity might be, as we can put it, temporally deep, in the sense that growing beyond it might take depths of time of the sort that science forces us to accept as real, or as going-to-be-real. (This is a bit ironic, given the new atheists' emphasis on science.) In all that time, might entirely new capacities reveal to us a transcendent reality? Who knows?

It's not hard to see, therefore, that the immaturity view presses us away from a sweeping and totalizing religious denial or disbelief (or irreligious belief) to the very thing that we might otherwise have impatiently rejected as unduly timid: agnosticism. By seeing this, we see another example of how the framework for religious discussion focused on immaturity that we set up in Chapter 5 can be put to work. From the improved perspective it allows, we should evaluate religious agnosticism positively.

But we're not talking about the old agnosticism. This is a *new* agnosticism.

THREE LEVELS OF REASONABLE DOUBT

The new agnosticism will jump out at you if you think through the conclusion we reached two chapters ago – which is to say that it makes perfect sense in the context of the immaturity view. It's part of the weight I said my three-legged stool would hold. But we need to have a good close look at it. When we do, we'll see that it consists of three levels of doubt, stacked together.

I'm going to present these three in such a way that it's clear my main aim in the book so far has been to convince those to *only* doubt, religiously, who might otherwise have been inclined to take a more negative line – that is, to disbelieve in a perfectly general way. My main aim is not to convince those who are now religious believers to be agnostic about religion instead. This is in line with what I mentioned in the prologue, where I said that I was especially interested in communicating with the religiously disaffected, the Nones, many of whom disbelieve religiously in that perfectly general way or are so inclined. Another way of putting my point would be to say that I'm mainly seeking to bring disbelievers up to agnosticism, not to bring believers down to it.

The first level of the new agnosticism is the one we get to when, thinking within the framework established by the immaturity view, we grant that no judgment as to religion being unsuccessful over the long haul, unable to make contact with a real transcendent reality, is reasonable at the present time. Though we often presuppose that we're mature enough to see that much, we should instead be in doubt about it. Here we're just noting a pretty obvious implication of previous work.

We start moving to the second level when we notice an important *connection* between this claim we're now in doubt about and another one – the claim that all religious ideas are false. Here's the connection: *If* all religious ideas are false *then* religion will never be successful. The new claim, as can be seen, depends for its believability on the believability of the claim we've just found ourselves in doubt about. Note carefully that with "all religious ideas" the new claim isn't talking just about the triple transcendence ideas we know about or those that are parts of claims found in religion up to the present – as we've seen, these claims could all be false and yet religion could still be successful in the future because of the later emergence of new and more plausible religious possibilities. Maybe everything we've seen so far in religion represents no more than the early stirrings of the human religious impulse. Only if all known *and also all unknown* religious ideas are false do we get the connection I'm talking about here, to the idea that religion won't ever be successful. So when saying "all religious ideas are false" in the present context, that's what I mean.

Assuming that's clear, let's move on and see how we get all the way to the second level of doubt. What we've said in making the connection just mentioned is that if all religious ideas are false then religion will never be successful. But remember that we're in *doubt* about religion never being successful instead of agreeing with that idea – that's what happened at the first level. So we have to also be in doubt about the notion that all religious ideas are false. That all religious ideas are false is not something it's reasonable to believe; instead we ought to leave the issue open. If it *were* reasonable to believe that all religious ideas are false, it would also be reasonable to believe that religion will never be successful, since (because of the connection) the second idea just follows from the first. But we have to be in doubt about the second idea. So we have to be in doubt about the first one too. We should be agnostic about it.

And now we can notice something else, something structurally similar to the move just made. We can bring in a third important proposition taking us to the very center of irreligiousness, namely, that that there is no triply transcendent reality, and observe that *if* there's no triply transcendent reality *then* all religious ideas are false. These two notions are connected in the same way the other two were. Putting it another way, approved by logic: If any religious idea is true then there has to be some transcendent fact of the relevant kind. Maybe not about God or a god or any other thing imagined by religion so far. But something. Otherwise we wouldn't yet have a religious idea, according to the assumption about religion's nature governing this book. (Remember Chapter 1.) Indeed, you can take the connection both ways in this case. Though the two propositions are different, they are mutually entailing: If there's no triply transcendent reality then all religious claims are false, and if all religious claims are false then there's no triply transcendent reality. So if we're in doubt, agnostic, about whether all religious ideas are false, as we were persuaded to be at level two, then *because* of this connection we have to be – it would be unreasonable not to be – agnostic as well about there being a triply transcendent reality. That there is no triply transcendent reality is not something it is reasonable for us to believe. And with that insight, we arrive at the third level of the new agnosticism. Up here, where one can see a long way, what we see is that we have to be open to there being a triply transcendent reality and so, quite conspicuously, open to the heart of religion being real instead of an illusion.

Of course my metaphor of moving from one 'level' to another is a bit misleading. The new agnosticism embraces *all three* levels. One way of bringing them together would involve noticing your condition when you've reached the third level. Now you can look back and see all three at the same time, and see how they fit together. You're agnostic about there being no triply transcendent reality because you're agnostic about all religious ideas being false. And you're agnostic about *that* because, having read the previous chapters of this book, you're agnostic about the claim that human religion will never be successful.

Here's a picture of the three levels:

(3) There is no triply transcendent reality.

⇓

(2) All religious claims are false.

⇓

(1) Religion will never be successful.

Though you're moving up from level 1 to level 3, coming to be in doubt about each proposition in turn, the arrows point down because they signal your discovery of an 'if-then' or 'only if' logical connection that starts at the next level up. Level 2's claim is true only if level 1's is too. But you've come to be in doubt about 1's claim. And so, because of the logical connection, that doubt has to transfer upward. And the same thing takes you up from 2 to 3.

Here's a scenario with exactly the same relationships that's intuitively easier to understand:

(3) John won the race.
⇓
(2) John entered the race.
⇓
(1) John paid the admission fee.

John can enter the race (level 2) only if he paid the admission fee (level 1). Suppose you're in doubt about his having done that. Then because of the 'only if' connection you'll also be in doubt about whether he entered the race. And John certainly can win the race (level 3) only if he entered it (level 2). So, having come to be in doubt about whether he did enter it, you'll also be in doubt about whether he won the race. The 'doubt transfers' are the same.

BUT WHAT EXACTLY IS DOUBT?

So now we have, as a possible intellectual attitude, not just the old agnosticism. We also have this new agnosticism: reasonable doubt about the three interlocking propositions about religion we've been talking about. The new agnosticism, as it happens, is compatible with the old: maybe you're in doubt specifically about whether there's a personal God as well as generally about whether there is some transcendent reality. But one cool thing, as suggested earlier, is that the new agnosticism is also compatible with what we might call the *old atheism*, the traditional view of philosophers who have *denied* the existence of God. The new agnosticism leaves open the possibility that there is a triply transcendent reality, but that reality need not be God. It might be something that only becomes recognizable to us much further down the road. So one could rule out God while remaining a new agnostic. It's only if you rule out every actual and possible religious claim that the latter avenue isn't open to you.

In this section I want to deal with something else we need to get clearer about – just what do we mean when we talk about doubt? This is the attitude of the new agnostic, and indeed of anyone who's agnostic about anything. (Though the notion has come to be tied to religion, and that's going to be our focus, we can speak of 'being agnostic about' the claim that we have free will or about whether the big bang really started it all or indeed about any claim or proposition whatever.) This doubting feature of agnosticism is the one that makes its critics among the new atheists think of it as so namby-pamby. When we look closely at it, however, it seems to come down to little more than an absence of belief either way on some issue you've been thinking about – for example, the absence both of the belief that there is and of the belief that there isn't a triply transcendent reality. Because to know something you have to believe it, this absence of belief further means an absence of knowledge on both sides – which helps to explain why agnosticism is so often associated with 'not knowing.'

But here we should pause to distinguish doubt of the sort in question, which removes belief (and thereby knowledge), from *doubts*, in the plural. You can have your doubts about something – which is to say, questions tending to make you a bit less confident – even when you believe it and are overall confident that it's true. You might, for example, have some doubts about whether there's a God while on balance believing that there is. Lots of people do. To be clear about this, we can say that the doubt of the agnostic amounts to being *in* doubt, where being in doubt about a proposition you've thought about is, again, just to lack a belief either way.

We can also put this more positively: The doubt of the agnostic means that she's intellectually open on both sides of an issue. This might not be namby-pamby at all. Perhaps it's really hard, since everyone seems to have made up their mind, and you're feeling social pressure to conform; but you think they're jumping to conclusions and so you follow the pressure of your own brain. What you can also see here is that the absence of belief in the agnostic's case is generally the result of other beliefs – beliefs, for example, about the quality of the available evidence. So if we want either the old agnostic or new agnostic to believe, here's a news flash: she does! It's just that what she believes on the one hand supports not believing on the other.

I've been saying a lot about belief, that is, about the *attitude* of belief – which is to say of believing. It may have occurred to you that when defining doubt in terms of (the absence of) belief, we really incur an obligation to say something about what belief is. If this is your view, then you're assuming that what belief is isn't clear, and I could just respond by saying you know very well what it is, since our beliefs are available to us through introspection. Of course you have to catch yourself in the act.

That expression – 'catch yourself in the act' – actually raises an issue about believing that I do want to attend to. When you catch yourself believing you'll see that it's *not* an act: it's not something you can do, just by trying. Try right now to believe that Donald Trump was never an American President. Go ahead – try! You can't do it. Why? Because believing is something that comes over you – it's a bit like depression or joy that way – when the world seems to stand behind a proposition (of course other things, like your wishes, can make the world seem to do so). And for most of us there's nothing that will make the world seem to stand behind the proposition that Trump was never President. Though arguably not the same as a feeling of confidence – I mentioned these two in the same breath earlier – believing is *like* such a feeling in being involuntary. And the two go together in this way: If you gain enough confidence about a proposition you will also believe it; and if you lose enough confidence you will cease believing. This itself shows that belief is involuntary. For if it were voluntary it wouldn't be vulnerable in this way to being lost.

Now maybe you'll say that the proper candidate for voluntary do-it-yourself believing is something you could *go either way on*; it's then that whether you believe is up to you. Well, pick something and try it! Maybe the idea that there are alien intelligences on one of those interesting exoplanets astronomers have been discovering will do. You won't be able to believe it just by trying. It won't work. At least it won't if what you call belief is what I call belief. The experience of believing I have in mind just isn't like that; it's an involuntary *sense* that something is true or is the case rather than an action or anything that could be the immediate result of an action. (And notice that it isn't being able to imagine something as true or being willing to bet on its being true or anything like that either.) Clearly we have such experiences of sensing. And they're what the experience of believing, as I'm understanding it, will give you.

Now there's something in the same neighborhood that you *can* do voluntarily, and maybe it's because this is hanging out close by that we can get confused about the nature of belief. You can *mentally judge* that something is so. To make a judgment is generally to do something. Same thing here, though it's usually so swift and easy, such a natural accompaniment of believing, that we don't catch ourselves in the act. Judging that a proposition is true means performing a mental act of endorsing it as true or acknowledging it as true in response to evidence that convinces you, mentally 'taking sides' with that proposition when considering what's true. Generally, as I've said, when you come to believe something, you also judge that it's true. Upon consulting the evidence you involuntarily have the sense – believe – that someone is guilty of a crime, and you also mentally acknowledge what the evidence shows, filing away the belief that she's guilty with all the other things you regard as true and plan to treat accordingly. But you don't have to do this. Suppose that 'she' is your wife, and the crime is a stabbing. For a long time your attachment to your wife prevents you from even believing that she did it – that is, blocks the sense that it's really true. But the evidence is overwhelming, and at a certain point you can't help believing. At this point you still have a choice as to whether you'll judge that she did it. It would be too great an act of disloyalty, so you don't. Of course I'm not saying that you consciously and deliberately think all of this through. Our psychological life doesn't work like that. And I don't mean either that you're just deciding not to act on your belief out in the world – by going to the police and telling them what you know, for example. That might be true too, but if so, it's something that happens after the mental judgment is withheld. The latter act is further back, psychologically speaking.

And now we've stumbled on a notion you may be somewhat familiar with: the notion of *withholding judgment*. Actually, I planned this, since, especially in philosophy, the attitude of the agnostic is often described in precisely those terms. Writers who say that the agnostic withholds judgment will frequently think of withholding judgment as being identical to the not-believing we were talking about a bit earlier and so to being in doubt, or as necessarily coinciding with it. But what we've seen more recently suggests that there's another possibility we need to be sensitive to. It could be that you do believe something because that's just how the world strikes you, but you *still* withhold judgment. The notion of withholding judgment can only do any really distinctive work for us if we allow for this interpretation; otherwise belief and judgment are just blurred and pretty much treated interchangeably.

To apply this to the new agnosticism, maybe you came into this discussion believing that there's nothing triply transcendent at all, and after seeing all the evidence supporting doubt about this proposition, you still believe it. Because belief is involuntary, there are all kinds of ways this could be made to happen. But even so, how you believe and judge the *evidence* to be may lead you to withhold judgment as to whether there's something transcendent or not. You mentally back away from an idea you believe! Of course, typically your belief will soon depart too, so long as the evidence continues to look to you as it does. But the point here is that even if it doesn't, no judgment on the issue at hand need be rendered.

Should we say of someone like this that he's an agnostic – a new agnostic in our case? I think we should. Accordingly I will understand the new agnosticism broadly enough to cover this sort of case. I'll still keep talking about the agnostic's attitude in terms of doubt, though. This is, after all, the usual case, and even the person who withholds judgment while believing will allow that there's a sense in which he should be in doubt. Moreover, it would be awkward to always say "doubts and withholds judgment or else withholds judgment though believing." But you've been put on notice that that's what I regard as the truth about the attitude of the agnostic.

OK. So now we know what the new agnostic is agnostic about, and also what sort of mental attitude goes with being agnostic about something. The new agnostic is in doubt about whether there is no triply transcendent reality (and this because she's in doubt about whether all religious ideas are false, which in turn is supported by doubt about whether the basic human project of religion will never be successful). And of course we're aware of how closely the new agnosticism is tied to our results in the first half of this book, and in particular how natural and obvious it should seem in the context of the immaturity view.

Suppose you understand and accept all that. You'll be able to see how such agnosticism fits well with the new relationship between science and religion encouraged by the last chapter. What I want to consider now is how it should lead us to new thoughts about the not-unrelated claim – a claim that has become quite popular in our time – of metaphysical naturalism.

8

Naturalism Tamed

What I want to show in this chapter is that, given the force of the immaturity view and the imperative represented by the new agnosticism, it isn't reasonable to believe metaphysical naturalism to be true – at least when it is formulated in such a way as to oppose religious ideas. I'm not saying we should regard the claim as *false*. For all we know, it may turn out to be true. But in circumstances of religious immaturity it is not the fierce threat and danger to religious ideas of transcendence that, in our culture, it is commonly thought to be. In particular, it is not *so* serious a threat that we should reformulate religious ideas to make them *compatible* with naturalism, as various contemporary religious thinkers appear to suppose. Perhaps this will all change after the human religion project has been given its due, but for now naturalism is tamed.

The basic reason for this is that belief in naturalism involves thoughts about religion that are quite premature. Our religious immaturity, as we've seen, gives the idea of transcendence a new lease on life. And this means that naturalistic belief comes up wanting. In this context we will once again encounter the new atheists, and see why their view is problematic. Atheism as such might be a reasonable belief, and elsewhere I've argued that it is. But it can be a reasonable belief only insofar as it gets itself disentangled from *naturalistic* belief.

WHAT IS METAPHYSICAL NATURALISM?

The way the word 'metaphysical' is used here means that 'naturalism' concerns *reality* or what there is, and what there most *fundamentally* is. (It's important that the word is 'metaphysical' not 'methodological':

methodological naturalism is quite different, involving only the policy of assuming that natural explanations will be found for whatever you're investigating when doing science.) Consider the human body. It consists of many different things and many different types of thing all working together marvelously – except, of course, when you're sick or when you die – in ways you can learn about from some elementary study of human anatomy. Muscles, tissues, blood, bones, nerves, cells. That just begins the list. But at bottom there's just *one* thing, one kind of reality: namely, physical reality. Your body is a physical thing, all the way down to the sub-atomic level. That's what it most fundamentally is. In the same way we can think about and try to answer the philosophical – the metaphysical – question about what *everything* most fundamentally is. You can, in other words, enlarge the scope of your investigation to the whole of reality. (Or to the whole of concrete reality: to get a view opposed to religion we don't need to worry about what naturalists would regard as the proper view of abstract things such as numbers and sets.) This is obviously a pretty ambitious undertaking, but one view you could come away with if you undertook it is the view called metaphysical naturalism.

What view that is can perhaps best be exposed by contrast with a more familiar metaphysical view, which in theology and philosophy is called *theism*. This is the view that a God exists, and when combined – as it is by believers – with the view that there is a natural world, you get a kind of *metaphysical dualism*, a view according to which reality is composed of two fundamentally different things stuck together somehow, in this case through God's creative act. So for theistic dualists, there's God and there's the natural world. For naturalists, though, there's only the natural world. That's it. That's the whole shebang. This is what naturalists claim. Metaphysical naturalism is therefore a kind of *monism* (one-ism) instead of a kind of dualism: it says that all reality is at bottom one kind of thing: natural.

So what does it mean to say that something is natural? Good question! Let's distinguish two answers. The first I'll call the System View. It holds that what makes something natural is that thing being part of a system of regularities of the sort we call 'natural laws.' Naturalism, on the System View, says that all of reality is such a system, it is a single system of natural law. The second option accepts what the first has said but wants to say more. I'll call it the Physical System View. Those who take this view say that it's through science that we're becoming acquainted with natural laws, and since the realm of science is the realm of the physical, the natural system should be regarded as a *physical* system. Without over-simplifying too much, we can get a sense of the Physical System View by saying that proponents of this view would take the example of your body from a moment ago and just keep going, claiming that what your body most fundamentally is, everything most fundamentally is. All reality is physical reality.

Of course contemporary physics is showing us how weird the realm of the physical and thus nature can be. But Physical System naturalists would hold that nature can't be *so* weird as to include things that aren't physical at all. By contrast, proponents of the more spare System View say there's nothing in the very idea of nature to preclude the non-physical. (Most, of course, still think science *in fact* supports a physical picture of things.) Suppose a non-physical and immaterial god-like being were discovered. According to John Searle, a well-known philosopher who accepts the System View, so long as the behavior of such an entity were regular and could be woven seamlessly into the system of regularities we already know, it would count as natural and be part of nature. Of course the gods of religion as we've known it so far – including God – tend not to be subject to natural law in this way. They're independent of natural regularities, doing their own thing. Indeed, in the case of God, we have the idea of a *creator* of nature. That's why many such beings are rightly called *super*natural even on the System View. The Physical System View obviously has an extra reason to regard them as supernatural, and indeed a good reason to regard all gods as supernatural entities, because such beings would be non-physical, and its version of naturalism holds that nothing in nature is.

Now of these two, it's really only the Physical System View that unequivocally opposes all ideas of transcendence. Only it gives the reality referred to by each such idea something to transcend! Searle's is a bracing notion, but it would make some religious ideas that are clearly ideas of transcendence compatible with naturalism. Take, for example, Spinoza's, mentioned at the beginning of the previous chapter: Spinoza's reality infinitely transcends what any naturalist would suppose to be real, yet it is a single deterministic system. Thus if we want to work with a form of naturalism that can mount a *general* challenge to religion, we'll work with the Physical System View. And in fact this is the popular view, the view rooted in science, that everyone is talking about when they say that naturalism threatens religion. Consider, for example, all those who speak of the 'causal closure of the physical' – the notion that everything physical has a physical explanation, which is commonly set against religious views about transcendence, such as the view that there is a miracle-working God. Accordingly, nature, for us, will be physical nature, and naturalists will be those who think that all of reality is a physical system.

HOW THE IMMATURITY VIEW OPPOSES
NATURALISTIC BELIEF

Having arrived at a clear view of the sort of naturalism that will be relevant in this chapter, it won't take long to see how someone working within the framework represented by the immaturity view must reject naturalistic belief. (Again, she won't say naturalism is false; just that it isn't reasonable to believe it.) Indeed, we're really just adding a fourth level to the new agnosticism, following the pattern from the last chapter, when we do so. With the third level, we arrived at a consideration of the claim that there is no triply transcendent reality, and we saw how the immaturity view leads to agnosticism about it. But now notice that the claim 'naturalism is true' (where by naturalism is meant the Physical System sort of naturalism) entails that there is no triply transcendent reality. Given that a triply transcendent reality would transcend the realm of the physical, if there is *only* that realm – if that's all of reality – then there is no triply transcendent reality. It can't be otherwise; this connection must hold. But immaturity gives us a good reason to be in *doubt* about, to be agnostic about, the claim that there is no triply transcendent reality. This we saw in the previous chapter. So in the same way that we moved from level to level there, we now can move up one more level, to doubt about whether naturalism is true. Because of the logical connection between the two propositions, the believability of the claim *naturalism is true* depends on the believability of the claim *there is no transcendent reality*. And so the fact that the immaturity view prevents the latter from being believable means that it prevents the former from being believable too.

Someone may now say that this was too easy. A view that for so long has been a pain in the neck for religion can't be deprived of its teeth quite so readily! My basic reply is that what we see here is just the hidden power of a properly developmental approach to religion, which teaches us about our developmental immaturity in matters religious. What we should be trying to understand is how these things could have *been* hidden from us. And our work in the first half of this book – together with Chapter 6 – suggests an answer. We've become puffed up by our special talent for science, incautiously supposing that this makes us universal geniuses, able to discern the lineaments of all reality. Here's another way of putting the point. Our success in science has made us think we're intellectually mature in quite a general way, and so has led to the supposition that everything to *follow* in the way of intellectual discovery in our future will be of the same sort. In fewer words: we've become biased. And of course the bias is a naturalistic bias. At the same time, we've been noticing everything that's going wrong in the religious dimension of human life, including in its intellectual domain. Popular ideas about God and gods we have found reason to regard as deeply flawed. Without our hubristic bias, this might only have made us think that, although good at science, we're bad at religion. We might have said: "Hey, it could take 10,000 years or more to see whether we can get anywhere in *this* dimension of life!" We might have seen that inferring the truth of naturalism was jumping to conclusions, and avoided getting so used to the idea that naturalism is a serious threat to religion. But instead, because of our hubristic bias, we assumed that religion was wrong-headed and going nowhere, and that nothing better would ever be forthcoming from religious activity – which allowed the bias to grow and allowed naturalism to assume its presently dominant cultural profile.

It may be that parts of this explanation aren't quite right, but it serves my present purpose, which is just to help us see how easily a developmental approach to religion could be moving in the right direction and really powerful *without us having noticed this*.

The defender of naturalistic belief may persist, however – as we should want her to, so we can be sure we've given her view a fair shake. What she may say is this. "You've shown that because of the connection between 'Naturalism is true' and 'There is no triply transcendent reality,' if we're reasonably in doubt about the latter, we should be in doubt about the former too. But by the same token – because of the very same connection – it's open to the naturalist to *start* from naturalism and, seeing that it entails that there is no triply transcendent reality, conclude that that's what she ought to believe."

For this sort of move to work, however, the naturalist would have to start off with good reason to believe naturalism. And the problem is that the arguments that might supply such a reason tend to assume or presuppose that the immaturity view at which we arrived in the first half of the book is mistaken, which means that they beg the question: They take for granted just what they're supposed to prove, and so in the present context don't amount to good arguments.

Let me illustrate. Suppose the naturalist says that the success of science should lead us to think – not just for the sake of doing science but when doing metaphysics – that everything that happens in the universe has a physical cause. Suppose this is her reason for being a naturalist and rejecting religion. (Recall that the third sort of transcendence has to do with benefits for us, here in our corner of the universe, that allegedly have a *transcendent* source; the naturalist putting forward such a claim might be expected to have her eye on this.) We could reply that 'everything' is a bit immodest here. But a stronger reply will point out that even if everything that happens in the universe has a physical cause, it could be a transcendent factor, further back in the causal chain, that makes those physical causes operate as they do. The naturalist needs it to be the case that *only* physical causes are at work in the universe, but this isn't entailed by her reason. Now suppose that this is added as an assumption, so that we really do have a reason for believing naturalism and rejecting religion. The assumption rules out all religious views, and so requires, to be any help at all, the further assumption that *human inquiry has arrived at a point where it is already possible for us to rule them out reasonably.* Just this the immaturity view would have us deny, however. So to make the naturalist's argument fly we have to assume as well that the immaturity view is mistaken. And this is when the bells go off and the red lights start flashing: That begs the question!

The naturalist may respond that it's neater and tidier, more economical and *simpler* (in the sense of non-complex), to suppose that, starting with physical causes as we begin explaining something, we'll be able to end with them too. And simplicity is a theoretical virtue. Indeed it is, I reply. But religious ideas might afford a different, higher-order simplicity of their own (here Spinoza's view may again provide an example). And in any case, simplicity can't come at the expense of explanatory adequacy. Now, maybe we don't know yet that there's something out there in reality that physical concepts won't suffice to explain. But this, in a way, is just the point. We don't know *yet.* Indeed, we may never know, and the reason may be that there *isn't* anything like that. But we're not anywhere close to being in a position to say this, precisely because of our religious immaturity. This has led to developmental delays – for example, in the careful exploration of a range of ideas about transcendence – which mean that we're now at quite a disadvantage when it comes to being able to say with any confidence that there's nothing transcendent that *would* require for its explanation the introduction of other than physical concepts. If the naturalist just assumes that there's nothing like that, she's again begging the question against our earlier results instead of providing a decent argument against them.

The upshot is that scientific arguments for naturalism are, in the present context, weak instead of strong. Naturalistic belief is, I'd suggest, in the end more closely tied to a cultural movement, or the zeitgeist, than to any argument. The reason that many people today are believing metaphysical naturalists (whether they would recognize the label or not) has to do with the enormous cultural success and prestige of science. Science is truly amazing. And of course what science is good at is charting the regularities of nature. With religion in many parts of the culture apparently in retreat – because, face it, religion so far is not all that amazing; remember here what we saw in Chapter 4 – science has come to dominate, culturally speaking. As Richard Rorty once wrote, in terms of moral heroism "the scientist replaces the priest." It's easy to imagine that science can and will ultimately tell us about everything, and since science studies nature, that means nature is everything. Presto: you've got metaphysical naturalism. But by now it should be clear how this train of thinking can and should be interrupted.

CONSEQUENCES FOR THE NEW ATHEISM

And this brings us back to the new atheists. The new atheists might better be called anti-religious metaphysical naturalists. They are, most of them, moved by the zeitgeist to be naturalists in the scientifically optimistic way, and because they see that naturalism rules out religion, and because religion as known in some parts of the world (for example, across broad swathes of America) has anti-scientific tendencies, the new atheists have become ardently anti-religious as well. I'd suggest that even the academics among them – for example, Richard Dawkins, Daniel Dennett, and Jerry Coyne – are frequently behaving as activists rather than as religious (or even anti-religious) thinkers. They would probably not have given religion a thought were it not for the way it keeps on getting up in their face about evolution! This means that something has to be done, and they mean to do it. But these sorts of motivations are seriously in tension with an aim of impartial truth-seeking about religious possibilities. Though the new atheists present themselves as on the side of reason and truth, their minds are made up in advance just as much as those of traditional religious folk.

So what should we expect from them in relation to arguments for and against the new agnosticism? Perhaps not much. Activism is one thing; careful intellectual thought another. One might even hope that activism such as theirs, opposed to anti-scientific tendencies among the conventionally religious, would be successful. Such success would have its place in moving us forward from our present religious immaturity. What I suggest we should want to see, however, is a clearer distinction being made between religion as we know it now in some parts of the West and religion as part of the human religion project, sprawled across time.

Here some reflection on evolutionary time might be relevant in a way the new atheists had not expected. But this won't happen until we see an end to the genuflecting before the zeitgeist. The latter yields a naturalism far more optimistic than it has any right to be, given that it is also largely innocent of argument. From metaphysical naturalism anyone can see that the falsehood of every religious idea, known and unknown, immediately follows. So there is absolutely no motivation, so long as we're in thrall to the zeitgeist, to imagine our religious immaturity and think positively about the future of religion. If the attachment to naturalism were even somewhat weakened, and 'anti-religious' came to be qualified as 'anti-antiscientifically-religious,' we might see the new atheists *really* becoming interested in reason and truth and investigation where religion, more broadly construed, is concerned. And to such a weakening, and to such a qualification and new interest, people continuing the intellectual efforts represented by the immaturity view and the new agnosticism might realistically aspire.

Perhaps it may help somewhat in the attempt to produce such results if we notice that atheism as such – or at least atheism as philosophy construes it – is not threatened by the immaturity view; only the *new* atheism which has got itself all entangled in naturalism is thus threatened. Indeed, in another book I have argued that when we take a good close look at certain aspects of human immaturity, particularly our moral immaturity, we can discover a new way of *defending* atheistic belief. The intellectually respectable atheism I have in mind here, as suggested in the previous chapter, might be called the *old* atheism.

It helps to think about the old atheism in relation to the old agnosticism. The old agnosticism involves doubt about whether there is a personal omni-God, an ultimate creative being with all knowledge, all power, and all goodness. The old atheism, as I understand it, denies that there is: it's the belief that there is *no* God. Just to keep clear what's being denied or doubted in these various cases, let's organize things under the two basic religious possibilities that are relevant here, the one broader and the other narrower:

There is a triply transcendent reality
Naturalistic belief denies this.
The new atheism (closely tied to naturalism) denies this.
The new agnosticism involves doubt about it but not denial.

There is a God
The old atheism denies this.
The old agnosticism involves doubt about it but not denial.
The new agnosticism is compatible both with doubt about this and with denial.

As noted in the last chapter, you can deny that there is a God while leaving open whether there is a triply transcendent reality: The idea of an ultimate *personal* being represents just one way – perhaps one we should expect to be especially attractive early on in the development of the religion project – to fill out the notion of triple transcendence. So the old atheist can quite consistently also be a new agnostic.

Of course the old atheism calls for careful development and argumentative support just as much as any other view about religion. As noted, I've tried to provide this elsewhere. I certainly wouldn't say that someone who combines the new agnosticism with the old agnosticism instead of with the old atheism has to be unreasonable. The immaturity view doesn't require you to be an atheist. But it does leave it open as a possibility – if I'm right, even a possibility that can be integrated with immaturity thought and the idea of progress for the religion project. And in this it is rather unlike most other views you may have heard of that give aid and sustenance to the defense of religious ideas.

CONSEQUENCES FOR *RELIGIOUS* NATURALISM

Most people, I expect, would find the idea of blending naturalism and religion into naturalistic religion a bit counterintuitive – something like blending a horse with an octopus. How could something be both a horse and an octopus at the same time? How could something be both naturalistic and religious? But this early in the religion project, we should be open to the idea.

In Chapter 1 we actually saw a way of giving it some plausibility. Cro-Magnons doing their religion thing, whatever it was, back in the Upper Paleolithic wouldn't have had the concept of nature or – therefore – the concept of transcendence. Science hadn't been invented yet. But we can still understand how they could have been doing something properly called religious, someone may say, by applying the concept of the transmundane. Though, no doubt, they didn't have the word, they will have had the concept. Even a Cro-Magnon could distinguish between the ordinary and the non-ordinary, the familiar and the unfamiliar. And this distinction can be made from within a contemporary scientifically souped-up naturalistic worldview too. That's pretty obvious, since science is constantly telling us about physical facts that are pretty weird, far from ordinary. And often not just weird, but wondrous.

Of course religion has gone through considerable changes since the Upper Paleolithic, as you'll rightly remind me. For a long time, the most influential religious ideas have emphasized transcendence, not just transmundanity, and this sets up the whole cultural standoff between naturalism and religion that has led us to this point. But some will say that it's precisely to *overcome* this standoff that ways of blending naturalism and religion need to be explored. If they could be made successful, we might be able to accept the best from both science and religion, and without resisting the naturalistic ethos that has gained such cultural power.

A recent example of this effort in philosophy is the work of Donald A. Crosby on what he calls a "religion of nature." This religion of nature invites us to recognize and honor what is ultimate – which for Crosby, a metaphysical naturalist, is nature – while engaged in "a search for values and modes of awareness that can provide basis, orientation, and direction for the whole course of our lives." Our values, according to Crosby, can be informed by nature because nature is itself intrinsically valuable in impressive ways that can be linked to the concept of the 'holy' or of the 'sacred.' Like many other religious naturalists, Crosby also links religious values more specifically to the demands of environmental ethics. In this way religion gains a connection to another powerful movement in our current culture, and potentially could become a force for good in the world rather than ill.

I myself think there is room in the religion project, most broadly conceived, for the exploration of such ideas. Let many flowers bloom! So my point here will not be that this approach has to be mistaken. My proposal, though, is that, under the most plausible interpretation, it too is in a certain sense *premature*. And this is another powerful, culturally relevant consequence of the immaturity view. Most attempts we've recently seen to develop a religious naturalism or a naturalistic religion appear to be premised on the thought that *transcendently oriented religion has failed*, or, more specifically, that *transcendently oriented religion must be rejected if we are to be kind to nature*. And, of course, there is also the rather important background thought that *naturalism has succeeded and should be believed.* The problems faced by the latter thought we have identified earlier in the chapter. The first thought we saw in the previous chapter to be undermined by the immaturity view: in its place we have put the first level of the new agnosticism. The thought in between seems, like the rest of what religious naturalists generally have to say about transcendently oriented religion, to depend on the idea that transcendently oriented religion as we've seen it so far represents the best that religion can do – another notion that is immediately cast into question when we see the force of the immaturity view. Moreover, as we'll see in Chapter 10, it's not hard to imagine how transcendent ideas could help environmentalist programs flourish while also supporting powerful and generous ethical impulses. Indeed, in some important respects *only* such religious ideas can do so.

The upshot is that all the urgency with which religious naturalism tends today to be defended drains away. Allowing the future into our deliberations in a manner that our humble hominin brain resists, using our *imaginations* and not just memories of the past, we can see that the immaturity view – as I put it at the beginning of this chapter – gives the old idea of transcendence a whole new lease on life.

So what should we do with our newfound freedom in the spiritual realm?

9

Agnostic Religion?

You might think it an unfortunate thing that the idea of triple transcendence should receive a new lease on life just when we're forced, by the same circumstances that provide it, to be agnostic about whether the idea is true. Even if the idea of transcendence gets a new lease on life, religion itself – and here we're back to talking about robust, transcendence-friendly religion – apparently doesn't. But notice what you're assuming. You're assuming that religion in an age of immaturity should have the same basic attitudes it's always had. And that seems highly questionable. Sure, religion *as we've seen it so far* is full of detailed conviction and passionate belief. It's tempting to suppose that this is how things have to be in the religious domain. Call this view *believerism*. But if there's anything we've learned, it's not to take religion as we've seen it so far to be representative of religion, period.

Religion, along with the rest of the human religion project, is as we've seen quite immature. And what if religion's conviction and passionate belief are often part of that very immaturity? What if, moreover, the evolution of a new form of religion compatible with the new agnosticism would be just the ticket for helping religion grow up? Then believerism would be false. Then we'd have a successful contender in the quest for what I've elsewhere called evolutionary religion – by which I mean *whatever* form or forms of religion *fit* or are well adapted to an early, immature stage of human religious development. If you look back at where we've been in the book, considering carefully what we've learned, you'll see that these ideas, defended in the present chapter, aren't nearly as outlandish as they may sound. Instead we're encountering some more of that power of a developmental approach to shake up our thinking about religious matters.

Now, don't take what I've said the wrong way. Agnostic religion would no doubt feature its own beliefs – scientific, moral, aesthetic, and so on – and these beliefs might often and appropriately be held passionately. It's just that it won't include the passionate belief that there is a triply transcendent reality or any other more detailed belief dependent on that one. Again, we're talking about a form of religion that starts from the stance of the new agnostic, as described two chapters back.

Could such a form of life be genuinely religious? And could it go anywhere? We'll have to see. I begin, though, by suggesting that another type of agnosticism needs to be added to make this form of religion fully available to the Nones in my audience and fully suited to an immature stage of religious development.

MORE AGNOSTICISM?

You may think that what I've said about agnostic religion so far already makes it a tall order, but I'm now going to make things even more challenging by adding as a prerequisite the possibility of being religiously agnostic in yet another sense: agnostic as to the more detailed nature of any triply transcendent reality there may be. I say: the *possibility*. We don't have to stipulate that everyone who participates in agnostic religion is doubly agnostic – maybe there'll be new agnostics taking part who think they have a pretty good idea as to what at any rate some features of the divine would be. But we need to leave room for others too.

The second agnosticism I have in mind here isn't of quite the same sort as the one we discussed earlier (that's why I call it 'second'), not only because it addresses the nature rather than the existence of a transcendent reality but because it isn't directed to a particular proposition, with the relevant belieflessness a lack of belief on either side of that proposition. You might think it's *each* proposition offering a description of what a triply transcendent reality would be like, if there were one, about which this extra sort of agnosticism is agnostic, but that won't work: There are plenty of detailed descriptions one may regard as false and so disbelieve even if one believes no such description to be true. Think about descriptions of gods perched on top of Mount Olympus in Greece. No, here we're indeed talking about a not-believing (and so a not-knowing), and that's why I'm willing to use the term 'agnosticism,' but it's a not-believing of a different and simpler kind. It's *not having a belief as to what a triply transcendent reality would be like* – apart, of course, from being triply transcendent.

Lacking belief in this extra sense means that one lacks something that's rather common in religion as we know it. For religious people are generally willing to say quite a lot about the detailed nature of the transcendent! They may, for example, tell you that the triply transcendent reality is a loving person-like being who acted to create the world and also to save it by becoming, for a time, a human person in the form of Jesus, who died for our sins. Of course in some forms of religion as we know it there is more reticence about providing details: that's the case, for example, in some forms of Buddhism and even in some more mystically oriented forms of Christianity. But as you might expect, given that we have these names to distinguish its traditions, today's religion generally wants to say *something* about the divine or sacred in addition to the claims (usually left implicit) about transcendence. So by adding this second form of agnosticism as at least a possibility, we are taking the new form of religion to be explored here even further away from religion as we know it – which might seem to add only a new threat to any identification of agnostic religion as religion.

So why do it? For three reasons. First, notice that among the Nones are many so-called apostates, who were once conventionally religious – good church-going Baptists, say, or practicing Hindus – but who have left the fold. And often this is because they simply don't find the detailed beliefs of their tradition credible anymore. Sometimes they don't find the detailed beliefs of *any* conventional form of religion credible. So if agnostic religion were not able to be doubly agnostic in the way I'm proposing, it wouldn't have any room for these Nones.

A second reason is that many of the arguments I used to build our immaturity framework and support the new agnosticism in earlier chapters do double duty, justifying also this extra agnosticism. For example, the bad record of past religion, surveyed in Chapter 4, suggests that religion would need to clean up its act before any details it might come up with could be regarded as reliable. The special challenges religion faces because of its big ambitions and our humble talents, discussed in Chapter 3, might similarly be used to suggest the unreliability of what we've come up with so far. Not to mention the new facts about deep time surveyed in Chapter 2, which should suggest to us that we might be way off in our assessment of how long it would take to reach enlightenment on such matters, if ever we do.

The third reason is connected to the second. It says that, given our present religious immaturity, we ought to spread our investigations far and wide, exposing every detailed picture of transcendent things we can for careful inspection, just so we don't miss the truth about which details are right through premature specification of what we think they would have to be. And this it will be much easier to do if there's room in agnostic religion for the second agnosticism.

So the two kinds of agnosticism both come quite well recommended. I'm at any rate going to try to find room for both. But can anything properly called religion actually accommodate both?

KEEPING RELIGION TRANSCENDENCE-BASED, BUT TRADING BELIEF FOR IMAGINATION

I say yes, and I say that's so even for the more metaphysically robust sort of religion I've had in my sights since the beginning of this book, which isn't ready to shut off talk of transcendent things in favor of only getting together for potlucks and bingo. (I stress 'only' because I don't want to suggest I've got anything against potlucks or bingo.) To support this stance I'm going to argue that religion could, at all relevant points, trade belief for imagination while remaining authentically religious.

As is well known, religious believers can frequently be found mumbling the relevant phrases or shuffling through the relevant physical movements without giving much thought to what they're saying or doing. Now suppose that on one of these occasions, our believer – let's call him Bob – is struck by a flash of imagination and starts contemplating what things really would have to be like for the words he's saying or singing to be true and for the actions he's doing to have the meaning assigned to them in his tradition. Indeed, Bob is struck so hard that he's overcome with wondering awe. What's more, Bob continues to use his imagination in this way during religious practice, and never shuffles or mumbles again. Now tell me: Does this change leave Bob at about the same level religiously or make him more religious?

I think we'd have to say it makes him more religious. But if that's so, then why should it be any derogation from religiousness, as opposed to an alteration or even intensification of it, if Bob starts imagining what it would be like for *other* pictures of transcendent things – pictures from traditions other than and even contrary to his own – to depict reality, finding himself again in a state of wondering awe, though also moved to be in doubt about his own tradition's details? Or if, with similar results, he divests the picture he's contemplating of any familiar details drawn from the world's religious life to date, replacing them with new transcendent possibilities he is able to imagine? Or leaves out *any* details, humbly allowing that humanity may not yet have evolved to the point where it is able to conceive divine details worthy of the imagination-induced wonder and awe he feels, and contemplates triple transcendence alone?

Now Bob, you'll say, has changed. He's not the Bob we knew! But has he changed in a way that leaves him non-religious? It certainly doesn't seem so. No – he's religious all right, just in a different way. Imagination has religious power, and is able to compete successfully with any belief that has you thinking these or those religious details are the right ones. Indeed, it can keep you authentically religious even when your beliefs about such matters have all gone away.

But, you'll want to remind me, not *all* Bob's religious beliefs have gone away. Presumably, though we've now contrived to have him in doubt as to the detailed nature of the transcendent facts, Bob still thinks there *are* transcendent facts. Bob still believes that there is a triply transcendent reality, and his imagination operates, as it were, on top of this belief. That's how it can have religious power. Otherwise, it wouldn't.

Well, let's see about that. Given what we've learned in previous chapters, we should certainly be ready to find out that this isn't right – that this part of believerism is just another prejudice about religion based on the sorts of religion we've most frequently encountered in the past. And I'm going to argue that this is indeed the truth of the matter. Again, I'll do so by showing how imagination can substitute for belief – this time where the belief is the belief that there is a triply transcendent reality.

The long and the short of it is that there is a kind of imaginative *faith*, which can be faith that there is a transcendent reality. This kind of faith can be built on top of the doubt of our new agnostic, even if not on out-and-out disbelief. It may presuppose many beliefs – such as, just for example, the belief that a triply transcendent reality would be wonderful – but it doesn't need the belief that there is such a reality. It simply does the faith thing differently. And in part because doubt still allows serious wondering and also wonder, it can be an authentically religious faith.

So much for a preview of what's to be seen here. Let's now look at this new kind of faith more closely. I'll proceed in two short stages. First we'll notice how faith that such and so can manage just fine without belief that such and so. And then we'll see how it can operate with imagination instead.

The idea of religious faith without religious belief is becoming more and more common in the philosophy of religion. But we don't need philosophers to sanction it. Ordinary experience will do. Try a little thought experiment. Suppose you've lost your ten-year-old son. The police fear he has been taken and killed. Days of searching have turned up nothing. Do you still believe that your son will be returned to you safe and sound? It wouldn't be surprising if you don't believe this – if this belief, which you were really thankful for at first, has been ripped away by everything that's happened. Of course you may not disbelieve. But at some point you will at least land in doubt. You can't help it. It's only human. As we saw in a previous chapter, belief – "the sense of reality," as William James called it – is involuntary. And negative evidence of the sort you've got here at some point will simply take your belief away.

But now let's shift gears slightly. Can you, in these circumstances of doubt and nonbelief, still have *faith* that your son will be returned to you alive and well? It sure seems that you can, if you lack clear evidence that he's dead. This too is only human. Indeed, it's only human in these circumstances to display a dogged faith that holds on to the idea that, somehow, all shall be well. Now is when you most need faith, to sustain your morale and motivate the continuation of the search and perhaps also to be true to your son. Here, one almost wants to say, we see faith's *raison d'être*. So surely it must be possible to have faith toward a proposition such as "My son will be returned to me safe and sound," even when you don't believe this proposition. And if the story makes sense with this proposition, why not with others, including religious propositions?

So you can have faith without belief. But with imagination instead? Yes, certainly. There may be more than one possible substitute. But this is one of them. Remember how, in the thought experiment, you found a way to 'hold on to the idea' that somehow all would be well? We didn't elaborate. But now let's notice how imagination can provide a way to do that. Imagination allows you to picture your son alive and well, and you hold on to the idea by deliberately doing so. You picture your son emerging from the cornfield. Or you picture him asleep in the arms of one of the searchers. Or you picture future experiences with your son. You might also just think to yourself "He's alive" without mental pictures. By imagining I here mean deliberately producing for yourself what psychologists and philosophers call a 'mental representation,' and mental representations aren't always literally pictures. Otherwise how could you mentally represent to yourself, assuming I haven't convinced you yet, that imagining doesn't require picturing? What picture would go with that? But back to you and your (imaginary) son. Imagining that your son is alive takes work. And if it turns into real faith, that's because you've formed the intention to be guided by this deliberately produced mental representation on an ongoing basis – to 'think by it,' as it were – and have succeeded in doing so. And to some extent you're also able to 'feel by it.' For example, instead of being really agitated you're able to calm yourself down, and thus you're able to help keep others calm too. Of course, at some point even this sort of faith would become unreasonable and indeed hardly possible, psychologically speaking – say, if conclusive evidence of your son's death turns up. (Imaginative faith goes well with doubt but not with disbelief.)

In a manner similar to what we've seen here by means of this thought experiment, one can mobilize the imagination in faith that there is a triply transcendent reality. Of course you can't picture this in any literal sense. Nonetheless you can contemplate what it would be like if that proposition were true, just as Bob contemplated what a change it would make to the nature of things if such and such a tradition's 'picture' of the divine were true. (Notice that when we described the Bob case we used the notion of a picture in this way but obviously didn't mean it literally.) Belief too involves having, or being disposed to have, some kind of mental representation. But when a believer thinks of there being a transcendent reality, a mental representation of this is involuntarily formed in the characteristically beliefy way. In imaginative faith, one deliberately represents the world *to oneself* as being such and so, and of course one also 'holds on to' the idea in the manner described above.

But by now we should expect to hear from the critic. Isn't this just some kind of silly pretense or make-believe – or alternatively a sad form of wishful thinking? Well, wishful thinking is actually a way of keeping a belief when the evidence is against it, and that's what makes it sad (when it is sad). It's belief caused by desire, generally by means of self-deception. In imaginative faith you instead acknowledge that the evidence is what it is. And then, in this completely clear-eyed condition, you add to your psychological state, which includes this knowledge, a layer of imagination and the other mental behavior mentioned earlier; you do not conspire to subtract your awareness of anything. So, no, imaginative faith isn't a form of wishful thinking. And it isn't pretense or make-believe either. When as a child you make-believe or pretend that mud cakes are real, you don't actually believe this, and neither do you just doubt it: you positively disbelieve it. (Suppose a mother says to her girls when their father is lost in a storm "Let's pretend that Daddy's ok." That wouldn't be very encouraging!) But in imaginative faith – as was already suggested in the earlier thought experiment – you don't disbelieve; you're only in doubt. Because you're only in doubt, the truth of the proposition in question remains a 'live option'; it could well be true. And so, for one reason or another, you imagine that it is. If it's shown to be false, your brain will let you know, and the whole point of having faith in the way you did will disappear.

What we see here is that such imaginative but agnostic faith isn't some kind of fictionalism – it's not just a matter of losing yourself in a mental world as you do when engrossed in a good novel. Again, that would be make-believe. Imaginative agnostic faith is instead going out on a mental limb for something you regard as really great or important and still seriously possible. It's because its truth would be important and remains seriously possible that you don't give it up. But if you transition from doubt to disbelief, that possibility has been taken away, and although you might still say its truth would be really important, you're more likely to say it would *have been* really important, for now you regard the notion as false. You stuck with it as long as it was reasonable to do so, and in a reasonable way, but the whole point of doing so is now gone.

Another question a critic might have for us regarding imaginative religious faith is whether it requires the *judgment* that there is a triply transcendent reality. Two chapters ago we saw that the new agnostic, strictly speaking, neither believes nor judges that such is the case. To have imaginative faith, doesn't she need to re-enlist the mental judgment, even if belief stays behind? And if so, is she truly an agnostic anymore?

Here an answer comes by recalling that a judgment of the sort in question is the judgment that some claim is *true*, and it is made as a response to what seems like strong evidence. The husband from our example in the earlier chapter, whose wife was charged with a stabbing, has to prevent himself from making a judgment that would normally be elicited as a result of powerful evidence; he does so out of loyalty. Another example: You're on a jury and can't help believing the defendant innocent – there's just something about him – but because the evidence proves his guilt beyond a reasonable doubt you nevertheless mentally judge him guilty. You count this as true because of the evidence even though you can't yet believe it. Imaginative faith doesn't feature anything like this, since it's when the evidence is relatively *weak* that, in certain circumstances, such faith is adopted as a replacement for belief. Such faith has got to be appropriate for situations in which, precisely because there's no strong evidence of the sort that would call for it, you withhold judgment.

At this point it would be good to note that while you remain agnostic and keep such faith – and in the case of religious faith, because of our immaturity that might well be one's long-term condition – much of the activity formerly supported by belief is still psychologically available to you. In our thought experiment, the parent of the lost boy, should she or he have imaginative faith, might behave much as he or she did when belief remained, now with this alternative means of support. And a person of religious faith can still behave as Bob did. Imagination, again, has religious power, and now we see that it has a kind of fully independent religious power. One can indeed imagine that the transcendent is real *in order* to engage in Bob-like behavior. One might do this, for example, because of amazement at the richness of religious metaphysical possibilities, or on account of this combined with a sense that it is imperative to improve on past religious investigation – which through serious religious activity just might in time yield evidence that such a possibility is real.

And many additions to Bob's behavior that stem from an imaginative faith stance rather than belief, ones sufficient to yield a full and rich religious life, could be mentioned. For example, you might continue to go to religious meetings and discuss with others the implications, for living, of there being a triply transcendent reality. And then you could go out and live that way. These meetings might be new meetings you arrange with like-minded others. But they wouldn't have to be. Sure, if you go to the religious meetings of established traditions, others there are likely to believe what you instead are imagining, and they'll have more details to draw on. (Even some of your fellow new agnostics may have more details if they're not doubly agnostic.) But you'll share with them the fundamental notion of triple transcendence. Everyone will be working with the idea of there being something beyond the wonderful world of nature that is even more wonderful, as well as liable to increase the fortunes of human life, ensuring that its depredations do not have the last word. And precisely because it's a *fundamental* religious idea, they will have to listen if you can show there are things that follow from that idea alone which they've been overlooking, because they were caught up in details. You could also think about the implications of triple transcendence for your own basic mental orientations: If you live by it, will you cultivate serenity, be less preoccupied with short-term goods, more willing to take risks for the good of yourself and others? The answers here seem all to be yes.

It would of course be silly to try to work out a lot of the details of agnostic religious practice. These, if they come to exist at all, will evolve out of actual attempts to get started on such practice, in circumstances that cannot be foreseen. But the more general points that can be made here and now are substantive and persuasive enough to show that something new is delivered by the immaturity view – a new form of religion *built specifically for immaturity* – that is worthy of our attention. And that will suffice for my purposes. One last general point to be added, in relation to religious immaturity, is the following. A form of agnostic and even doubly agnostic religion that trades belief for imagination not only remains authentically religious but also encourages doing many religious things *better* or more impressively and in maturity-enhancing ways, and so promotes growth beyond our present immature condition. For example, religion is supposed to encourage humility. Check and double check. Awe before transcendence. Ditto. In its major traditions, a wide inclusiveness. Ditto. Unity. Ditto. Religious faith is moreover supposed to be a virtue. Well, agnostic but imaginative religion gets rid of all the old problems about evidence, which have seemed to many to diminish faith's virtue, and it takes a lot more work than belief-based faith. Belief, as we've seen, is involuntary. Imagination is voluntary. So ditto again.

COULD AGNOSTIC RELIGION FLOURISH?

We've seen how agnostic religion, even in a doubly agnostic form, can be authentically religious. Believerism is false. But could such religion ever *go* anywhere? Could it flourish? Might not even the special voluntary quality just mentioned, which increases its difficulty, be an impediment to its success?

I'll argue that it could flourish. But again notice that a successful argument of this kind, given my purposes, need not speculate about how things will be in the future in any detailed manner. General considerations that support the view that agnostic religion can flourish, or even the view that there's no clear reason why it shouldn't, will do. Another opening point is that we should be clear about the form in which we want it to flourish. Do we want agnostic religion to take over the world, or dominate humanity's religious life in the foreseeable future? Is it supposed to flourish in that form? It might be hard to pull this off, needless to say! But I think it's clear that, in the present context, 'can flourish' would be supported in a relevant manner even if we showed no more than that it's not implausible to imagine agnostic religion, perhaps over some considerable time (remember the deep time frame of reference), beginning and growing into a noticeable presence in the context of human religious life – maybe one that functions successfully as an intellectual and spiritual gadfly.

Let me now make several points which, together, seem to me to show at least that much.

(1) First point. There are general reasons to engage in agnostic religion that could easily capture some nonbelieving people's interest and imagination. One of these is that agnostic religion can *aid religious investigation* of the sort we should all want to see succeed given the earlier results of this book. Awareness of our religious immaturity brings us many things, including a new reason to be religious: What better way to investigate religious possibilities? By living a religious life one might gain unique access to relevant facts, for example through special experiences elicited by religious practice or special insights yielded by its concentrated attention on spiritual things. A second reason was touched on earlier in connection with wonder: Humans are drawn in not just by curiosity but by wonder, and an imaginative form of religion affords plenty of scope for it. A third reason has to do with practical benefits that the efforts of imaginative religion might win for many, such as a greater zest for living as well as a structure for living that can make sense of, and unify, a highly diverse set of concerns. No doubt there are other general reasons of this sort. Some further suggestions, involving both these reasons and others, can be gleaned from the discussion of the next chapter.

(2) The second point I want to note concerns a particular discussion taking place today about whether traditional believing religions are best at providing the benefits associated with community, or whether purely secular communities can do the job equally well. Here agnostic religion offers itself as a *plausible middle ground*. Psychologist Michael E. Price (like many others) has emphasized how human religion makes possible "inter-generational communities who interact regularly and who share values and worldviews; networks of mutually supportive long-term relationships; opportunities for fellowship and social bonding; and ritual commemorations of life's most meaningful events." Religious notions of transcendence are hard to make up for in secular communities. In particular, Price notes the value of religion's ability to appeal to all kinds of people, to make members feel they're part of a force for good in the world, and to project gravitas. Well, precisely because of its agnosticism, agnostic religion won't appeal to the traditionally religious. But the latter already have their

communities, and the qualities associated with the new agnosticism might come to appeal to many secularists (more on this in the next chapter). And agnostic religion retains these qualities without giving up on transcendence, as we saw earlier in this chapter. Thereby it keeps the element of gravitas that was mentioned, as well as a profound mission: helping religion – and indeed all of us – to grow up. Thus, at least as far as fostering community is concerned, it might come to be seen by many seeking secular community as offering the best of both worlds.

(3) A third point draws our attention to a broader phenomenon involving religion, which we've already had occasion to mention several times: the rise of the Nones. Agnostic religion might come to be seen explicitly as *an alternative for the Nones*, which for one reason or another some of them take up. Earlier I mentioned those Nones known as 'apostates.' Other subgroups commonly distinguished include not only atheists, old and new, and the old agnostics, but also the 'liminals' (who are comfortable with neither a secular nor a religious identity) and the 'fuzzy fidelists' or, as we might say, 'somethingists' (who do not participate in conventional religion but believe there is 'something more'). Many of these people are on some kind of quest, and one with religious overtones. Agnostic religion, contextualized by the immaturity view, gives them another option to consider, one that can make sense of their quest. It is also a way in which groups of people quite consciously claiming the label of Nones could come to see themselves as religious pioneers – whose efforts signal, surprisingly, the *beginning* of religion rather than the end (contrary to what's sometimes said in connection with the Nones). I think this last consideration has the potential to capture the imagination of many Nones.

(4) Holding down the fourth position we have the following point. Agnostic religion offers itself as a viable *'next step' for religious progressives*, which some or many might wish to take. Religious progressives, unlike the Nones, stay in one or another traditional form of religion but try to enlarge it from the inside – and to push it in a more liberal and humanizing direction. In Christianity a prominent example is the late Marcus Borg. Others are Diana Butler Bass and Brian McLaren. But non-Christian religious traditions have their own progressives. Most are sensitive to the value of cultural evolution and have a healthy respect for science.

As such, religious progressives are fairly open to the sorts of considerations that, as we've seen in this book, lead to the immaturity
view. And thus the step to agnostic religion might, for many, not be
a very big step. Like the Nones, religious progressives are able to
find in the immaturity view a perspective that makes sense of their
own efforts. Unlike them, they have not given up on religion. This
combination makes the challenge of attracting them to agnostic
religion different but – or so I suggest – no greater than the (plaus-
ibly meetable) challenge we identified in the case of the Nones.

(5) A fifth point is that agnostic religion offers *a way to enliven and
reward liberal theologies*, which in many parts of our culture are
languishing in the doldrums. Think, for example, of the theologies
feeding mainline churches in America, whose populations shrink
while conservative and evangelical churches charge ahead. Liberal
theology gets criticized from many different quarters for being
allegedly vague and mushy or convoluted and obscure or timid
and compromising. Lately, even the new atheists have gotten in on
the act, accusing liberal theologians of moreover being evasive and
escapist, taking refuge in claims of mystery instead of just getting
off a sinking ship. Liberal theologians might be forgiven, therefore,
for having a religious inferiority complex. But agnostic religion
and the immaturity framework in which it is set could give them
a big shot in the arm. It reaches out to them, as it were, from the
future, suggesting that their unwillingness to say much about the
inner nature of the divine or to believe many religious propositions
is on quite the right track and can take the religion project to new
heights. If agnostic religion were to succeed, liberal theologians
might even regard themselves as having been prescient. (This is
why I used the word 'reward' above.) So there is much here that
might potentially attract liberal theology to agnostic religion.

(6) Finally, I'd like to mention the well-known *social power of common
attitudes*, which often allows things to change quite quickly from
what was previously expected. Of course, there are many other
things that can cause swift and unexpected change – an asteroid
might do it. But when people start thinking alike the phenomenon
can spread and reach critical mass. Thus who knows what might
happen if, as a result of such factors as the five just mentioned, a
fair number of people began to participate in some new way of
being religious like agnostic religion? I must say that this last factor
is not one I would absolutely count on in the present context. But,

especially in conjunction with the other points, it does support an openness to the flourishing of agnostic religion. It helps to support the view that the idea defended in this section is not implausible. And given our goal in this last part of the chapter's discussion, that's enough.

The New Humanism

When people of today, including the Nones, look back over the past life of our culture and ahead to the future, they often think that the perspective to take with us into that future is *secular humanism*. Secular humanism says religion has had its chance and failed. Or at least that it – secular humanism – can take the good things from religion, combine them with a bunch of other good things, and leave us ahead of the game. But the claims defended in this book show how religion can rise again. And the content of the argument, somewhat unexpectedly, suggests how a new religious humanism might be developed. Among other things, I want to give some attention to how strongly this new humanism challenges secular humanism. Who is best fitted to take us into the deep future? Who passes – or best passes – a 10,000-year test understood in *that* sense?

It's the power of our immaturity framework to support a new agnosticism and to make agnostic religion sensible rather than strange that lies behind the new humanism. But let me be clear about something, as we begin. I do not assume – and my arguments will not need to presuppose – that a new agnostic who goes for agnostic religion *has* to appeal to human values or claim the 'humanist' label when justifying such a move. It's rather that an appeal to human values represents a *possible* way to go – one I would indeed recommend (it builds in certain ways on some of the 'general reasons' for agnostic religion already set out in the previous chapter) – and when one takes this route the possibility of successfully defending a new religious humanism capable of displacing secular humanism quite naturally emerges. That it does so is one more significant cultural consequence of our developmental approach, to be added to the others we've been developing since Chapter 5.

SECULAR HUMANISM

As you might expect given the label, secular humanism is a general view that defines itself with one eye on religion, whose guidance it rejects, and the other on all things human, regarded very positively as all by themselves capable of generating meaning and purpose built on profound values. These values focus on the dignity and needs of human life and its long-term potential on the planet (sometimes in the universe), which secular humanists generally commit themselves to promoting in every way possible. Secular humanists sometimes concede that their liberal and progressive values owe something to religion's 'softer' effects in the West, for example, the compassion and selfless love associated with Jesus. Some also wish to preserve something of a religious ethos, gathering once a week and performing rituals; this sort of humanism occasionally even accepts the label 'religious humanism.' But for obvious reasons humanism (even without the extra label 'secular,' which for some will seem redundant) must seem incompatible with a more robust religiousness – with ideas about *transcendence* treated as important and quite possibly true.

An excellent recent discussion and defense of secular humanism, which I'll be dialoguing with, is the philosopher Philip Kitcher's *Life After Faith: The Case for Secular Humanism*. Getting better acquainted with its views will be a good way to deepen our understanding of a secular humanist position. Kitcher takes seriously a way of being religious – he calls it "refined religion" – that bears some similarities to agnostic religion, especially in its ability to manage without details about transcendent things. (It seems to reflect his conversance with liberal Christian theology.) Kitcher admirably tries, by taking them seriously, to do full justice to religious options before arguing for the superiority of secular ones.

But superior he does take the latter to be, primarily for two related reasons. First, he says, refined claims about the transcendent are nebulous and unreliable. Second, according to Kitcher, refined religion, like all religion, "identifies the transcendent as the source of values and virtues, ideals and duties" and thus displays a "commitment to values that are external to (independent of) the believer, and indeed to all human beings." The transcendent, in other words, "just is the ground of values" in even the most admirable forms of religion.

This view is mistaken, Kitcher thinks. Transcendent ideas make a poor basis for ethics and human progress. Rather, ethical values should be grounded in biological and cultural evolution, which features the growing sophistication of communitarian moral reasoning amid genuine moral progress. This needs no external standard to validate it. As Kitcher puts it: "I take the grounds of value to lie in the reasonings and conversations in which we engage with one another, as we struggle to cope with fundamental features of the human predicament, in particular with our existence as social beings whose capacity to respond to others is limited." Out of such work has come "nothing less than a transformation of human existence." There is thus no need for a "detour through some dim and remote transcendent."

As might be expected, secular humanists generally accept metaphysical naturalism (the view we discussed in Chapter 8). Though he allows that a bare possibility of truth may be conceded to the most refined religious propositions, Kitcher plumps for metaphysical naturalism too. As he says, his humanism is "concerned with the value of human lives in a thoroughly natural world." Refined religion may sometimes be an ally, and "a secular worldview ought to be forged in dialogue, even in passionate interaction, with all that has been most deeply thought about what it is to be human – including whatever can be refined out of religious traditions." So Kitcher's secular humanism keeps a friendly demeanor toward religion. But in the end, the problems with religious ethics and the plausibility of naturalism over transcendence lead him to see the best humanism as sponsoring "successors" to religion. These successors "will draw on a far broader range of cultural items – borrowing from poets and filmmakers, musicians, artists, and scientists, cultivating social institutions to develop the senses of identity and community traditionally fostered by religion."

TOP-DOWN OR BOTTOM-UP?

These thoughts from Kitcher – and so from secular humanism – are likely to sound quite reasonable. Educated readers, including many Nones, might be forgiven for finding all of this almost commonsensical, given their sense of the deficiencies of traditional religion. But let me now begin to show how the views developed in this book make a more interesting and much more competitive religious approach to all things human possible.

A basic distinction will be key – a distinction between what I'll call *top-down* and *bottom-up* religious approaches to things human, including human value. Let me explain what I mean. The approach Kitcher describes, which he assumes is essential to religion, including 'refined religion,' grounds all value in the transcendent. The transcendent reality, on this view, is the *source* of all value, and so of all human value. To figure out how to live and what matters in human life, we need its help; we can't do it on our own. This – you guessed it – is the top-down approach.

But this top-down feature which Kitcher thinks is written into religion is, I would argue, in fact quite optional for religious people. It's even optional in conventional religion – say, in God-centered religion. Some theists do think of God as the source of value, but many others don't. They think of value, including moral value, as autonomous. As the Christian philosopher George Mavrodes once charmingly put it, expressing this view, "morality stands on its own two feet, whatever those feet may turn out to be." Human beings without God, according to theists who take this line, can see that (say) love and justice are important and valuable, and precisely for this reason will think of God as just and loving. Value need not be grounded in transcendence even if a transcendent reality of the religious sort would be transcendent in value.

And it's here, I think, that we may be able to spot the confusion that commonly generates Kitcher's sort of view. It's a confusion of something we've seen *is* essential to religion – the idea that the transcendent reality is of greater importance and intrinsic value than anything in the familiar natural world – with something that isn't – the top-down idea that the transcendent reality is so special in relation to value that it is the *source* of all value. Simply put, it's a confusion of the idea that the transcendent is valuable with the idea that value is transcendent.

Avoiding this confusion, we'll better be able to see that religion can deploy the alternative, bottom-up option. And here I have in mind not just the sort of move mentioned above in connection with theists who use their own, autonomously derived standards of value to determine that an unsurpassably great personal being would be just and loving. I mean something bigger – something that will already begin to hint at the contours of the new religious humanism soon to be our focus. I mean that *reflection on what we independently value about human life can provide a basis for adopting a form of religion such as agnostic religion.* Bottom-up.

Let's suppose that some view like Kitcher's about the source of value is correct. And let's suppose also that all the things in human life that secular humanists say have value do indeed have value, just as they say they do. Starting from here, making use of these things, I want to say, we can justify agnostic religion. A religious orientation, in other words, can evolve out of a due appreciation for human values. When this happens, you get a genuine religious humanism, by which I mean a two-layer view with facts about us at the bottom and claims about how real, transcendence-based religion best allows us to do justice to those facts at the top.

So it turns out that Kitcher's 'refined religion' is less refined than it might be. Open reflection and wide experience of the sort that generate it – the sort of thing you see in (or that is presupposed by) liberal and progressive theologies – can take religion a lot further. Or at least they can if they see the point of working within the immaturity framework central to this book, which gives to questions about human needs a distinctive twist while at the same time making us quite content with a much less confident attitude regarding things religious.

DEFENDING (AGNOSTIC) RELIGIOUS HUMANISM

By noticing that a religious approach to human value doesn't have to be top-down we remove one of Kitcher's main objections to such an approach. His other main objection was to the seeming nebulousness and unreliability of claims about the transcendent, once they have been refined to the point where traditional arguments against religion (for example, arguments against the existence of a personal God) can no longer get a grip. But this is neatly dealt with by applying resources available to the immaturity view, as suggested near the end of the previous section. At an immature stage of religious development we will be religiously agnostic, and so don't need the 'reliability' naturally required for *belief*-worthiness. And we should *want* things left open and comparatively nebulous, because it's way too early to have a lot of details; we need to be motivated to explore many actual and possible ways of filling out that general idea of triple transcendence as we seek to improve on the poor-quality religious investigation of the past. In any case, the notion of triple transcendence isn't nearly as lacking in content as Kitcher's arguments against refined religion might lead one to think. As we saw in the last chapter, consequences for action can be derived from it. We need to strike a balance here, with an eye to the needs of religious practice but also to facts about religious immaturity. And the idea of triple transcendence – *more* bare than most conventional religious ideas but not actually bare – can be seen as allowing us to do so.

So Kitcher's objections to any approach of the sort I'm developing are, I think, well answered from within our immaturity framework and with the right information about the options available to religion when it comes to thinking about value. But we also need a positive defense. We need to show how the bottom-up approach can work and work persuasively with humanist values and agnostic religion, thus generating a new religious humanism. I will now sketch such a positive defense.

To get it, as suggested earlier when I described the two-layer position that the bottom-up approach would yield, we'll have to try to show how a religious approach, and in particular agnostic religion, better does justice to facts about human life and human values than a secular approach. So now the competition mentioned at the beginning of this chapter begins. Humanists tend, as we've seen, to be quite interested in the future of human life. I want to make sure that we're all interested *enough*, with due acknowledgment of deep time and of how the challenges to human life and values may multiply as we move much further into the future. And that's why we can – in the new sense of the present chapter – call this competition the 10,000-year test. It will be good to keep this in mind when assessing the force of my arguments.

THE VALUE-ADDED ARGUMENT

The first argument for an (agnostic) religious humanism I'm calling the *Value-Added Argument*. Agnostic religion, it tells us, will be able to offer us everything secular humanism can offer and *also* a whole lot more. Four aspects or emphases of this argument may be distinguished, which generate premises to support that conclusion.

Agnostic religion offers a positive way to structure or organize our lives, just as secular humanism does. The transcendent it imagines, being transcendent, is deep enough and also broad enough – since it embodies both reality and value – to provide a reference point for all one's activities, which may in the light of this idea be organized so as to promote further human maturing, growing up. (For details, see the previous chapter.)

This structure is capable of absorbing the best of what secularity has to offer. The emphasis on deepened human maturity, especially in the hands of the Nones, would converge with the values of secular humanism. Practitioners of agnostic religion have emotionally and otherwise achieved some distance from conventional religion, and their complaints against it are often humanistically based. They'll favor liberty of thought and behavior, and will want to listen to reason and to their humanistic impulses. Indeed, with a deep sense of human immaturity they will be open to learning from anything, anywhere. A basic assumption of any religious effort they undertake will therefore be the compatibility of the transcendent with the appropriateness of such an orientation.

Agnostic religion is at least as rationally satisfying as a thoroughly secular perspective. The old problem of faith and reason here simply goes away, since it is through philosophical discernment and scientific awareness that agnostic religion becomes possible in the first place, by people committed to reason's demands that it is practiced, and by arguments like this Value-Added Argument that it can become rationally justified. And precisely by being agnostic, agnostic religion avoids the problems we've seen attend religious belief – and also belief in metaphysical naturalism, a view that secular humanists generally buy into.

Agnostic religion moreover *responds positively to inimitably human impulses that secular humanism* cannot *satisfy and enables a unique moral response to the world.* Here we see the critical point that the evolving perspective on religion represented by agnostic religion can add something to what the best secular options have to offer. It adds at least the following three things, in particular.

First, with its expanded conception of transcendent possibilities, it permits for our most powerful and profound religious experiences a *non-reductive interpretation*. We don't have to suppose that their causes are fully accounted for naturally, in terms of micro-seizures in the brain, say. We don't leap to the belief that we've just been granted a window to the divine, either, of course. But we interpret them as potentially perceptual, and engage with them imaginatively and use them to broaden and deepen our conception of transcendent things even further, committing ourselves to doing so and to building on the results far into the future.

Second, a religious perspective, through the third emphasis of triple transcendence, also offers at least some hope of an afterlife and so *hope for the redemption of all those whom nature has destroyed.* After all, transcendent facts might allow for this. Secular humanism can offer hope for future people, who may be saved from suffering by our present and future efforts, if we are successful, but no hope directed to the past is possible under its auspices.

Third, the religious view enables *a tribute to – or an expression of respect for – human values that is not secularly possible.* The sayings and doings of a religious life allow us to treat the world as one in which all the human things that are for us most deeply imbued with value will achieve fulfillment, a fulfillment that without the truth of religious claims they would often be denied. The moral ideal of complete justice, for example, deserves our stoutest allegiance and respect whether there is a transcendent reality on the side of the good or not, but of course it may not be fully realized. In such a case, it is precisely because of how deeply something is valued quite on its own that the desire that there should be Something More to allow for its fulfillment is elicited. Living a religious life means living as though that will indeed happen. Collectively, religious sayings and doings can function as a uniquely extravagant and profound gesture or tribute to the value of what is most important to us, a tribute that one makes with one's life.

THE VALUE-IMPROVED ARGUMENT

The Value-Added Argument can work together with another argument, the *Value-Improved Argument*. According to this second argument, certain humanistic concerns that, on the basis of the previous argument, we might only have held to be at least as well accommodated by agnostic religion as by secular humanism are in fact *further* advanced by approaching them religiously. Precisely because of human immaturity, we need every bit of help we can get ensuring the survival and flourishing of the species over the next hundreds and thousands of years, and so, if a form of religion provides important extra assistance in this regard without lapsing into unreason, it should be preferred to a bare secularism. Again it will be helpful to elaborate, distinguishing the argument's main emphases.

The survival and flourishing of the species over the long haul is endangered. As is well known, we face many natural and humanly contrived threats. In particular, as various writers, including scientists such as E. O. Wilson and James Lovelock, have told us, we are currently despoiling the Earth. The human experiment is in some danger of ending in failure.

We should do all we can to improve the situation. It would be disastrous on many fronts were the human experiment to end in failure, so early in the life and culture of our species, and thus we have a profound obligation to do whatever we can to prevent this and to help realize, instead, the success of that experiment. Since so many other human goods prized by humanists and imagined for the future depend on this one, there is indeed a case for saying that the obligation seen here should be regarded by them as a *fundamental* obligation.

One thing we can do to improve the situation is to try to make religion work for us instead of against us. Conventional religion in a variety of ways is helping us despoil the Earth and closing our eyes to threats. The suggestion that we should try to make religion work for us instead of against us might seem quite desperate if conventional religion were representative of religion, period. But from within the immaturity framework we've constructed, the latter idea is quickly exploded. Religion might yet be made to work for us and for the world. With its emotional and social power, a more mature religiousness focused on facilitating maturity *generally* could indeed provide crucial motivation and support for work on a wide range of human problems that threaten our survival as a species, in essence becoming a central form of soft technology that offers a lot of help as we stumble toward the next century. Among other things, it would help keep the idea of progress before our minds, and provide additional structure and support for its realization.

If we develop and promote agnostic religion, we can achieve this goal. Agnostic religion – as we've indeed just seen in the Value-Added Argument – would be precisely the sort of religion that could do these things, thus working for us instead of against us. In the previous chapter we noted how it would provide a forum in which to cultivate serenity, become less preoccupied with short-term goods, and more willing to take risks for the good of ourselves and others. It would move us to behave rather differently from conventional religion in all relevant respects, and in particular more humbly, allowing us to be mindful of our human obligations and helping to organize all our efforts to fulfill them, while also providing a more optimistic and zestful environment for living of the sort that may be needed if we are, with full energy, to put our shoulders to the wheel. One centrally important feature of these points is the preservation of religious community, centered on robustly religious ideas. As we saw in the previous chapter, religious notions of transcendence are hard to make up for in secular communities. Religion, more easily than secularity, can appeal to all kinds of people, make members feel they're part of a force for good in the world, and project gravitas. Since agnostic religion would allow us to preserve all this, it offers vital support in the struggle for humanity.

SCORING THE HUMANISMS

In short, then, what the Value-Added Argument and Value-Improved Argument suggest is this: The new religious humanism should be preferred to secular humanism because, ironically, the religiousness it promotes even more deeply and effectively responds to humanistic impulses within the relevant deep time perspective, and thus is powerfully supported by such impulses. Humanism has sometimes sought to take over the best from religion, but many would say it has failed. Religion can aim to take the best from humanism and succeed.

But perhaps such triumphalism should itself seem a bit immature. So we can let this section be the shortest in the book. Though I've spoken of a competition and also, here, of scoring, I'm not as concerned to argue that the new religious humanism is ahead of the game as to make it clear that there is a fascinating new option here, one that helps to show how, given the resources reflected in this book, religion can be turned into a constructive force and, once again, can become a rationally and otherwise attractive option for mature human beings. If such a religious approach ends up working side by side with secular approaches and other religious approaches to promote vital human ends, so be it. At least there won't be as much fighting and bickering as the past has seen!

But how could any of these good things actually be realized? Here my thinking goes back to the Nones.

FROM NONES TO SOMES

If the reasoning of this book is successful, then religion can be revived and reformed in a big way by considering more deeply and imaginatively the very things – for example, the results of science and the needs of the future – that are leading people *away* from religion today. So religion deserves a second and third look from the Nones. Old evaluations should be reconsidered.

The Nones have looked at conventional religion long enough; its problems are legion. Arguments showing the vulnerability of belief in God might be cited by all Nones, but atheists, old and new, will be especially likely to have taken note of them. The old agnostics will be bothered by the problem of conflicting religious beliefs and by what CSR is suggesting about an evolutionary bias in favor of personal or agent-based religious concepts; liminals by the hard time conventional religion has providing anyone with a source of identity that welcomes everything good in the culture; apostates by such things as intolerant behavior in the church or synagogue or mosque; and somethingists by the insistence of conventional religion in the West on the acceptance of specific but scantily supported doctrines and creeds, and perhaps also by its resistance to non-Western religious influences. Nones in general will favor more freedom of thought than has yet become common in religious precincts, and bemoan the frequent substitution of religious authority for reason and basic humanitarian impulses.

Agnostic religion might have its own problems, but these are not likely to be among them. It allows us to imagine a more perfect union of rational, humanistic, and religious impulses than the world has yet seen. Under its auspices, Nones would be freed to think in many new ways about what transcendence-oriented religion might be. It may take some time to get used to this new freedom and to recognize fully that it is still *religion* we see where it's exercised. But, as noted in the last chapter, it is only a contingent fact that religion in the West has always featured detailed ideas about transcendent realities and firm beliefs as to their truth. We can imagine other ways things might have gone, with clarity from the very beginning of religion's history as to our immaturity and a humility to match. Forms of life focused on triple transcendence that developed from such a beginning would still have been religion.

Agnostic religion, therefore, is taking one or two or sixteen steps forward, but, paradoxically, it tells us that we best move forward, religiously, by treating ourselves as much *less* advanced than we generally think we are, and developing a kind of religiousness to match. At our present stage, it's enough to emphasize the notion of Something More. The 'more' here, as we've seen, though it may sound slender, has some solid content. It is more both descriptively and evaluatively: The transcendent is more than nature at the level of raw fact but also is imagined as more impressive and beautiful, even if we have not yet learned to appreciate many of the facets of its beauty. This 'more' may be contrasted with the 'less' of pain, suffering, meaninglessness, as well as the immaturity so often involved in their production. Human minds will naturally rush to fill in detail. But such instant gratification needs to be resisted, so that a new delight in the core religious idea and in the variety of ways in which it might be elaborated and applied, including many we have not yet conceived, can be cultivated. We need a picture with enough content to be religious but one that doesn't come pre-defined or filled-in, which therefore can welcome a much wider and deeper set of spiritual and intellectual explorations than any conventional religiousness is willing to countenance.

The Nones might be expected to welcome all this and evaluate it positively. And they're in an advantageous position when it comes to making radical changes of the sort required to turn agnostic religion into a reality. They don't need to become convinced that religion, as we see it today, is mired in difficulties. They're already there. Moreover, the various problems they have with conventional religion are such that any new religiousness they bring into being would automatically be allergic to religious authority and its restrictions on liberty of thought and behavior. Their religiousness would naturally incorporate humanistic impulses. So were Nones to become relevantly convinced and motivated, radical change would not be long in appearing. What's really needed is for the Nones to give the difficulties and problems they associate with conventional religion a new interpretation – immaturity, not religion's best shot gone awry – and become motivated to think and feel and behave in more religiously optimistic ways.

That's why it's so important that we learn to think of religion as unfinished rather than as finished (in either sense). Serious imaginative reconceptualization is required. Many have assumed that if there is to be a religious option, it has to be represented by some old form or by a reworked version of conventional religion. It's been easy to reject the more broad and open ideas of a transcendent reality as escapist or empty. But the immaturity narrative as developed in this book takes care of all that. Suddenly Nones can imagine a next stage for religion different enough from what came before to allow them to be part of it.

If Charles Taylor is right in his big book *A Secular Age*, religion seeded the rise of humanism. Now, ironically, humanism can seed a return for religion. Instead of spelling the end of religion, humanism can help religion re-enter cultural evolution. What we can imagine now is a new way of being religious, free from worries about such things as the biological theory of natural selection and women in the priesthood. These threadbare debates are replaced by more relevant and interesting challenges. The question now is not what would the first-century Jesus do? More likely, it will be what would future enlightened and mature people think about such things as our prison systems, our practices of capital punishment and war, our relationship with the natural world?

And the new way of being religious brings to these challenges the very widest range of resources, which include the creation of a genuinely possible and practical relation to transcendence. This new approach is not arrogantly new or cultish, but – among other things – new in its humility, in its willingness to perceive and take account of our place in time. Such humility will help us all to see that religion, and the human world it has done so much to shape, have not got off to the best start. But in a world in which 10,000 years are but a day, that doesn't have to be an insurmountable problem or the final evaluation.

Epilogue: The Religion Project

When, under the broad influence of science, we ascend to the macro level and in a no-holds-barred manner treat religious inquiry developmentally, we set off a kind of chain reaction. Forced by such a move to consider what *stage* of development we're at, we arrive at the surprising conclusion that the religious dimension of human life is still developmentally immature. But if it's immature, then further surprises follow. For now we have to think in brand new ways about a range of interrelated and culturally important views with a bearing, often negative, on robust religion. The assumption that humanism is best and strongest when secular and the restrictive but seemingly obvious stance of believerism, along with praise of naturalistic belief, derision of religious agnosticism, and a host of popular views about science and religion fostering a negative evaluation of the latter – all these things have to go. Seeing this, we have the opportunity to change our orientation quite radically. We may now be motivated to turn the religious dimension of life into a great human *project* – like science in that respect, though in this case a project barely begun – and devote ourselves to the promotion of its further development toward maturity. Religious inquiry, coming into its own culturally after the rise of science, might still have its own chance to stand tall.

why ?

These are exciting results. But you may have noticed that it's only in the last of them, only in the final link in the chain, that we get an idea that's been with us from the beginning: the idea of the religion project. Precisely because of the oversights and mistaken presuppositions about matters of maturity that I've been flagging, we humans generally *haven't* yet been treating our religion-related activities explicitly as a project. Although I've been speaking about the religion project since the prologue to this book, and though I've sometimes made it sound like an established human phenomenon, long in existence, this feature is really designed to bring into sharp relief *a new possibility*. It's designed to help us see the whole religion thing in a different light.

And now we get to decide whether the light stays on. Since the illumination it affords is real, that shouldn't be a tough decision, even if it does mean a serious adjustment to fairly well-entrenched mental habits. Assuming we seriously want the truth of things, if the earlier links in that chain of ideas seem solid we can hardly abstain from making our own contribution to the forging of this last one. But it's still no foregone conclusion that this will occur. Immature our *religious life* will be regardless, but whether we think of this immaturity as the immaturity of a *project* is up to us. In this book I have invited us to do so. I have invited us to take on Religion After Science.

This invitation is addressed in a special way to the Nones. The silencing of believerism and the advent of a new religious humanism should make it especially attractive to those Nones who've found religion meaningful in the past; and the taming of naturalism, the enlarging of agnosticism, and the associated exposure of an interesting new way of thinking about the relationship between science and religion might be expected to recommend it to all Nones, including those whose former instinct was to oppose religion. If we accept the invitation, we will see differently the 50,000 years or so of religion-related activity we have behind us, and especially the last 6,000, when the most formative of religious events occurred. We will think of this as the period in which the species was *initiated* into the religion project. This initiatory experience has been attended by many difficulties, and, as one might expect, our footing has seldom been sure. The book has had a fair bit to say about that side of things, often under the label of 'shortcomings.' But all is far from lost. There is much further to go. The story of our work on religion has just begun.

Reflecting on the past, we can see how all the exciting results of the book – all the new insights that may raise the profile of religion, that give robust, transcendently oriented religion a future – are really just the surprising consequences of religious *neglect*. (For a while I thought about working this idea into a different subtitle for the book: "On the Surprising Consequences of Religious Neglect.") There's really a double neglect to be mentioned here. First, a general sort of neglect visible all the way back through the history of religion and religious inquiry, reflecting in part our lack of humility and tightly linked to what I've called immaturity as shortcoming. Second, there's also a more specific neglect (partly rooted in the causes of the general) that's more recent, going back to the beginnings of modern science, intensifying with the discovery of deep time and evolution, that has had many of our cultural elites trashing religion instead of thinking about how it might now be more impressively developed. The combination of these two forms of neglect enables a developmental approach, once it *is* applied, to have radical consequences, as it snips and casts aside all the anti-religious sentiments that have flowered in its absence, in the soil of that neglect.

And this developmental approach, with its reshaping and pruning, makes space for the religion project. What we're getting acquainted with here is an entirely new way of looking at things in the religious domain. It brings with it a chance to be part of something big, comparable to the beginning of modern science. Something pretty amazing is in our power – if only we can shift from memory into imagination long enough to see it.

Notes

Prologue: The 10,000-Year Test

p. 2: *My previous work on related topics.* See my *Evolutionary Religion* (Oxford: Oxford University Press, 2013). For a more detailed and comprehensive treatment of certain topics, see my Cornell University Press trilogy: *Prolegomena to a Philosophy of Religion* (Ithaca, NY: Cornell University Press, 2005), *The Wisdom to Doubt: A Justification of Religious Skepticism* (Ithaca, NY: Cornell University Press, 2007), and *The Will to Imagine: A Justification of Skeptical Religion* (Ithaca, NY: Cornell University Press, 2009).

p. 4: *The theologian and philosopher Friedrich Schleiermacher addressed a book.* Friedrich Schleiermacher, *On Religion: Speeches to Its Cultured Despisers,* Richard Crouter, trans. and ed. (Cambridge: Cambridge University Press, 1988).

Chapter 1 Development and the Divine

p. 7: *That was quite possibly erectus.* It may have happened earlier. But the cooking of food is traced back to around the emergence of *Homo erectus.* And the earliest strong physical evidence of the controlled use of fire is dated to the time of that species. See Francesco Berna, Paul Goldberg, Liora Kolska Horwitz, James Brink, Sharon Holt, Marion Bamford, and Michael Chazan, "Microstratigraphic evidence of in situ fire in the Acheulean strata of Wonderwerk Cave, Northern Cape province, South Africa," *Proceedings of the National Academy of Sciences* 109 (2012), 7593–7594.

p. 7: *That may have happened as far back as Homo heidelbergensis.* See Jayne Wilkins, Benjamin J. Schoville, Kyle S. Brown, and Michael Chazan, "Evidence for early hafted hunting technology," *Science* 338 (2012), 942–946.

p. 7: *Had to come up with a religious thought.* Even those who disagree with me about what goes into a religious thought will probably give the event similar evolutionary coordinates. More on this later.

p. 8: *Dreaming, with its odd and shadowy denizens and their strange behaviors, could generate such thoughts.* This idea, associated with the nineteenth-century British anthropologist E. B. Tylor and defended by Nietzsche, is discussed and supported more recently on the basis of a wide body of evidence by Kelly Bulkeley in *Big Dreams: The Science of Dreaming and the Origin of Religion* (Oxford: Oxford University Press, 2016).

p. 8: *And the relevant experts think religion has been around for at least as long as that.* The reason for the common reference to a time 50,000 years before the present is that about then much relevant physical evidence suddenly becomes available. For this reason, among others, some scholars have been inclined to think of earlier hints of religiousness as amounting to proto-religion. See Matt J. Rossano, "The religious mind and the evolution of religion," *Review of General Psychology* 10 (2006), 350. Moreover, religion has been believed to be bound up with other important and culturally relevant events, perhaps including the advent of language, occurring about 50,000 years ago. See, for example, John E. Pfeiffer, *The Creative Explosion: An Inquiry into the Origins of Art and Religion* (New York: Harper and Row, 1982) and Richard G. Klein, *The Human Career: Human Biological and Cultural Origins*, 2nd edn. (Chicago: University of Chicago Press, 1999). But my phrase 'at least' is important here. There is considerable controversy about when and how religion evolved. (A nice survey of much of this appears in Rossano.) And the idea of a 'human revolution' dating to about 50,000 years ago has recently been challenged, with its component events either pushed back several tens of thousands of years or viewed as occurring more gradually or both. See Paul Mellars, Katie Boyle, Ofer Bar-Yosef, and Chris Stringer, eds., *Rethinking the Human Revolution: New Behavioural and Biological Perspectives on the Origin and Dispersal of Modern Humans* (Cambridge: The McDonald Institute for Archaeological Research, 2007). It's noteworthy that the major late work on the evolution of religion produced by Robert Bellah takes these reassessments seriously and works with them. See Robert N. Bellah, *Religion in Human Evolution: From the Paleolithic to the Axial Age* (Cambridge, MA: Harvard University Press, 2011). Nevertheless, because the available evidence makes it safe, when I've needed a number in the text I've used '50,000.'

p. 9: *At least implicitly, quite widely accepted.* The notion of a transcendent reality (often called 'supernatural') is especially common, and so is the idea of special benefits. See, among many examples, Pascal Boyer, *Religion Explained: The Human Instincts that Fashion Gods, Spirits, and Ancestors* (London: Random House, 2001) and Scott Atran, *In Gods We Trust: The Evolutionary Landscape of Religion* (Oxford: Oxford University Press, 2002). The notion of transcendent significance is less commonly made explicit, but it is implicit in much that one does find, including the use of words such as 'sacred' and 'divine' and the emphasis on 'awe' and 'devotion' and 'ecstatic ritual' as well as on how, from early on, the transcendent reality was in many quarters regarded as the appropriate source of human morality. See – again from among many examples – Nicholas Wade, *The Faith Instinct: How Religion Evolved and Why It Endures* (New York: Penguin Books, 2009), pp. 10–15.

p. 9: *Including scholars of the deep evolutionary past.* I've mentioned a number already in previous notes. Rossano is a particularly clear example.

p. 10: *Something can be transmundane without being transcendent.* These two are often conflated. One who does not conflate them is Bellah. See *Religion in Human Evolution*, pp. 1–2.

p. 10: *I have argued elsewhere.* See my *Progressive Atheism: How Moral Evolution Changes the God Debate* (London: Bloomsbury, 2019), ch. 10.

p. 11: *More like those enabling intellectual advances through art.* Some of the ways this can happen are suggested in Regina Coupar, "Can art *be* theology?" *Toronto Journal of Theology* 28 (2012), 61–80.

p. 12: *There's no mystery about how change or evolution can be progressive ... if we have goals by which to measure our progress.* This simple point might be helpful in the often combative discussions of the relations between cultural evolution and progress. See Tim Lewens, *Cultural Evolution: Conceptual Challenges* (Oxford: Oxford University Press, 2015), pp. 35–37.

p. 13: *Providing orientation in life for individuals and communities.* For a recent work emphasizing orientation, see Ingolf U. Dalferth, *Transcendence and the Secular World: Life in Orientation to Ultimate Presence*, Jo Bennet trans. (Tübingen: Mohr Siebeck, 2018).

p. 14: *Even when we would regard them as fictitious.* Religious fictionalism has been receiving a fair bit of attention recently. For discussion, see Robin Le Poidevin, "Playing the God game: the perils of religious fictionalism," in Andrei Buckareff and Yujin Nagasawa, eds., *Alternative Concepts of God: Essays on the Metaphysics of the Divine* (Oxford: Oxford University Press, 2016), pp. 178–192.

p. 15: *The nineteenth-century French philosopher Auguste Comte.* Comte's view appears in the context of his law of three stages, the third of which is associated with science, as discussed in *Cours de philosophie positive.* This work was translated and condensed by Harriet Martineau as *The Positive Philosophy of Auguste Comte* (London: J. Chapman, 1853).

p. 18: *Amusingly, this seems always to have been the case.* What I mean is that even at the very beginning of religion, when one might most expect the fact of its bare beginning to be taken into account, such humility is absent. As far back as one can go in religious history and prehistory, all the signs are of forms of life laced with conviction, sure that a basic religious understanding is available fully formed (as it were) from the head of Zeus.

p. 18: *Where the empiricist Francis Bacon found science ... and maybe even where that other Bacon fellow, Roger ... found it.* Links between the two Bacons are explored in Herbert Hochberg, "The empirical philosophy of Roger and Francis Bacon," *Philosophy of Science* 20 (1953), 313–326.

Chapter 2 The End Is Not Near

p. 19: *In Time's Arrow, Time's Cycle.* Stephen Jay Gould, *Time's Arrow, Time's Cycle: Myth and Metaphor in the Discovery of Geological Time* (Cambridge, MA: Harvard University Press, 1987).

p. 19: *Playfair later wrote.* For the quotation, see ibid., p. 62.

p. 21: *A billion years at least.* For some recent support, see K.-P. Schroeder and Robert Connon Smith, "Distant future of the Sun and Earth revisited," *Monthly Notices of the Royal Astronomical Society* 386 (2008), 157.

p. 24: *A recent paper in Science.* Jordi Quoidbach, Daniel T. Gilbert, and Timothy D. Wilson, "The end of history illusion," *Science* 339 (6115), 96–98. My quotations are from p. 96.

Chapter 3 Big Ambitions

p. 27: *A Sartrean sense of the absence of the divine.* I have in mind Jean-Paul Sartre's own youthful experience – or 'intuition' – of God's absence, which made him an atheist. See "Conversations," in Simone de Beauvoir, *Adieux: A Farewell to Sartre* (New York: Pantheon, 1984), pp. 434–435 and Notebook 3 in *The War Diaries of Jean-Paul Sartre* (New York: Pantheon, 1984), p. 71.

p. 28: *According to a 1947 estimate.* Richard W. Lindholm, "German finance during World War II," *American Economic Review* 37 (1947), 128n12.

p. 29: *As indicated when the word 'ultimate' is used to describe their concerns.* If the emphasis on ultimacy extends across all three aspects of triple transcendence, as arguably it does in most contemporary religion, what we have is of course triple *ultimacy* and not just triple transcendence. In other work, I have given special attention to the proposition that there is a triply ultimate reality, calling it *ultimism*. The claim that there is a God, or theism, as usually understood, entails ultimism, but the converse does not hold. Hence one can affirm ultimism or embrace it in faith while denying theism – that is, while being an atheist. These are interesting philosophical facts. Analogous points can be made with the claim that there is a triply transcendent reality, which theism and ultimism both entail while it entails neither. This means that there could be a triply transcendent reality even if theism and ultimism are both false. In this book, because of its general interests and the breadth of the triple transcendence claim (as seen here), I am treating the triple transcendence claim as religiously fundamental. In more restricted contexts, where, for example, the question is how religion ought to be understood for philosophical purposes, I am still inclined to see an ultimistic emphasis as appropriate.

p. 32: *Why we survived when the weather changed sharply some 40,000 years ago though the hapless Neanderthals didn't.* Paleoanthropologist Clive Finlayson, in *The Humans Who Went Extinct: Why Neanderthals Died Out and We Survived* (Oxford: Oxford University Press, 2009), puts a lot of emphasis on luck and chance. But he also repeatedly refers to how we were often people on the edge, on the margins, and so needed inventiveness or innovation to manage the situations of life. And we used it to survive when – our luck? – the weather changed.

p. 35: *The late twentieth-century American philosopher William P. Alston.* See William P. Alston, *Perceiving God: The Epistemology of Religious Experience* (Ithaca, NY: Cornell University Press, 1991).

p. 35: *That even Alston realized it would be challenging to deal with.* Ibid., p. 255.

p. 36: *Alston suggests that what's needed is a massive transreligious "system of overriders."* Ibid., pp. 271, 278.

Chapter 4 A Poor Record

p. 40: *Nonbelief is often said to have its source in pride.* This sort of argument continues to be discussed among believers. See, for example, Ebrahim Azadegan, "Divine hiddenness and human sin: the noetic effects of human sin," *Journal of Reformed Theology* 7 (2013), 69–90 and John Greco, "No-fault atheism," in Adam Green and Eleonore Stump, eds., *Hidden Divinity and Religious Belief: New Perspectives* (Cambridge: Cambridge University Press, 2015).

p. 40: *Ludwig Wittgenstein once said.* Ludwig Wittgenstein, *Culture and Value*, Peter Winch trans. (Chicago: University of Chicago Press, 1984), p. 34c.

p. 48: *In his book Behave.* See Robert M. Sapolsky, *Behave: The Biology of Humans at Our Best and Worst* (New York: Penguin Books, 2017), p. 605.

Chapter 5 Verdict: Immature, Not Doomed

p. 58: *As an example, consider Ludwig Wittgenstein.* What I say about Wittgenstein and the philosophy of mathematics is based on Ray Monk's excellent biography, *Ludwig Wittgenstein: The Duty of Genius* (New York: Penguin Books, 1990).

Chapter 6 A New Path for Science and Religion

p. 66: *A recent article in Nautilus.* Michael Fitzgerald, "Atheism, the computer model: big data meets history to forecast the rise and fall of religion," *Nautilus* 045 (2017), http://nautil.us/issue/45/power/atheism-the-computer-model.

p. 66: *Thinking in the cognitive science of religion (CSR).* One of the most recent works in this still-young field of science is James Cresswell, *Culture and the Cognitive Science of Religion* (New York: Routledge, 2018).

p. 67: *Brain scientists Thad A. Polk and J. Paul Hamilton point out.* Thad A. Polk and J. Paul Hamilton, "Reading, writing, and arithmetic in the brain: neural specialization for acquired function," in Patricia Ann Reuter-Lorenz, Frank Rösler, and Paul Baltes, eds., *Lifespan Development and the Brain: The Perspective of Biocultural Co-Constructivism* (Cambridge: Cambridge University Press, 2006). Quotations are taken from pp. 186, 196.

p. 69: *As the British philosopher Richard Swinburne notably has done.* See his little book *Is There a God?* rev. edn. (Oxford: Oxford University Press, 2010), p. 2. The big book in which the job is really tackled is his *The Existence of God*, 2nd edn. (Oxford: Oxford University Press, 2004). Swinburne's own version of the fine-tuning argument appears there in ch. 8.

p. 70: *A stage of development something like science's in the Middle Ages.* Interestingly, I first encountered this particular thought – as I was led to recall by someone else's recent reference to it – in the work of a Christian writer. See Alston, *Perceiving God*, p. 278. Alston makes this comment when his back is against the wall in a chapter on the problem of religious disagreement. But he does not take his insight nearly as far as the insight itself – as distinct from Alston's more conservative aims in that chapter – would have us go. Even when he entertains the thought of future change leading to a new religious consensus, his assumption is that a personal God will be at the center of it. (You can see this on the same page.)

p. 76: *Will itself be replaced by the even more exciting and ambitious James Webb Space Telescope in a few more years.* www.jwst.nasa.gov/.

p. 77: *Stephen Jay Gould ... beloved science writer, came out with a book.* The book is *Rocks of Ages: Science and Religion in the Fullness of Life* (New York: Ballantine Books, 1999). His central phrase first appears on p. 5.

p. 78: *A book by the philosophers Michael Peterson and Michael Ruse.* Their book is *Science, Evolution, and Religion: A Debate about Atheism and Theism* (Oxford: Oxford University Press, 2016).

p. 78: *A typology made famous by Ian Barbour.* See Ian G. Barbour, *Religion in an Age of Science* (San Francisco, CA: Harper & Row, 1990).

p. 79: *At about the same stage of development, equally mature.* One or two warnings suggesting the differential application of such models in our history and so hinting at developmental themes have been sounded. See, for example, J. Wentzel van Huyssteen, *Duet or Duel? Theology and Science in a Postmodern World* (Harrisburg, PA: Trinity Press International, 1998), p. 3. But the larger developmental picture that allows us to imagine the religion project *as a whole* as being at an earlier stage, developmentally speaking, is not in evidence here.

Chapter 7 The New Agnosticism

p. 81: *A band of merry men, the new atheists.* Richard Dawkins, Christopher Hitchens, Sam Harris, and Daniel Dennett are usually regarded as the leaders of the movement. The attitude I describe in the text is most obvious in Dawkins and in his book *The God Delusion* (Boston: Houghton Mifflin Harcourt, 2006) and among those who regard themselves as – or at any rate behave as – his followers.

p. 81: *A term devised to describe himself by Thomas Huxley.* Huxley's claim about his invention appears in Leonard Huxley, ed., *The Life and Letters of Thomas Henry Huxley*, vol. 1 (London: Macmillan, 1900), pp. 319–320. The story – and the label – has stuck.

p. 81: *Darwin too claimed it.* Janet Browne, *Charles Darwin: The Power of Place* (Princeton, NJ: Princeton University Press, 2002), p. 391.

p. 81: *I have written books defending the view that there is no God.* See especially *Divine Hiddenness and Human Reason* (Ithaca, NY: Cornell University Press, 1993), *The Hiddenness Argument: Philosophy's New Challenge to Belief in God* (Oxford: Oxford University Press, 2015), and *Progressive Atheism.* By 'God' I mean the omni-God of personal theism. Reasons for restricting atheism's claim accordingly are offered in *Progressive Atheism.*

p. 82: *Which he would have called the real God*. This equivalence – "God or Nature" – appears in the original Latin version of Spinoza's *Ethics*: Baruch Spinoza, *Ethica*, in *Opera Posthuma* (Amsterdam, 1678), Part IV, Preface.

p. 88: *You can mentally judge that something is so*. In fact there are lots of things you can do – lots of distinctions in this neighborhood. This is nicely brought out in Kevin Mulligan, "Acceptance, acknowledgment, affirmation, agreement, assertion, belief, certainty, conviction, denial, judgment, refusal and rejection," in Mark Textor, ed., *Judgement and Truth in Early Analytic Philosophy and Phenomenology* (London: Palgrave Macmillan, 2013), pp. 97–136.

Chapter 8 Naturalism Tamed

p. 93: *According to John Searle*. See John R. Searle, *Mind, Language, and Society: Philosophy in the Real World* (New York: Basic Books, 1998), p. 35.

p. 93: *Those who speak of the 'causal closure of the physical.'* As, in many places, does Alvin Plantinga in *Where the Conflict Really Lies: Science, Religion, and Naturalism* (Oxford: Oxford University Press, 2011) and as do many science-based critics of religious belief; Plantinga shows this with numerous examples.

p. 97: *As Richard Rorty once wrote*. In "Science and solidarity," one of the papers appearing in Richard Rorty, *Objectivity, Relativism, and Truth: Philosophical Papers*, vol. 1 (Cambridge: Cambridge University Press, 1991), p. 35.

p. 97: *Frequently behaving as activists*. This can be detected not just in the rather one-sided defense of anti-religious views in their books, but – in the case of Dawkins and Dennett – in support for the Clergy Project, which offers aid and a voice for ministers who have lost belief in the supernatural (https://en.wikipedia.org/wiki/The_Clergy_Project) and – in the case of Coyne – in the content of online blogging (https://whyevolutionistrue.wordpress.com/).

p. 98: *In another book I have argued*. I have in mind *Progressive Atheism*.

p. 100: *The work of Donald A. Crosby on what he calls a "religion of nature."* Donald A. Crosby, *A Religion of Nature* (Albany, NY: SUNY Press, 2002). My quotation is from another book of his on related themes: *Living with Ambiguity: Religious Naturalism and the Menace of Evil* (Albany, NY: SUNY Press, 2008), p. 82.

p. 100: *Transcendently-oriented religion must be rejected if we are to be kind to nature*. This assumption appears also in a collection edited by Donald A. Crosby and Jeremy A. Stone, eds., *The Routledge Handbook of Religious Naturalism* (New York: Routledge, 2018). And here it is in an endorsement provided for this collection by Freya Mathews of Latrobe University: "Arguably, only by re-centring religious sentiment on the awe-inspiring workings of nature can the modern world shift to the earth-ethic that is so sorely needed in this era of ecological derangement. Science and philosophy have proved incapable of bringing about the needed value shift. Perhaps only religion, as has been well attested in recent decades, can move hearts and minds on the scale required. This book argues, rigorously and self-critically, for a religion of nature that might indeed, without sacrificing reason, begin to nudge us towards sanity and hope."

Chapter 9 Agnostic Religion?

p. 102: *What I've elsewhere called evolutionary religion.* See my *Evolutionary Religion*, esp. pp. 4–5, 73–74.

p. 106: *More and more common in the philosophy of religion.* See, for example: William Alston, "Belief, acceptance, and religious faith," in Jeff Jordan and Daniel Howard-Snyder, eds., *Faith, Freedom and Rationality* (London: Rowman and Littlefield, 1996); Robert Audi, *Rationality and Religious Commitment* (Oxford: Clarendon Press, 2011), ch. 3; Daniel Howard-Snyder, "Propositional faith: what it is and what it is not," *American Philosophical Quarterly* 50 (2013), 357–372; and Schellenberg, *Prolegomena to a Philosophy of Religion*, chs. 5 and 6.

p. 107: *"The sense of reality," as William James called it.* In William James, *The Principles of Psychology*, vol. 2 (Cambridge, MA: Harvard University Press, 1981), p. 913.

p. 109: *You're on a jury and can't help believing the defendant innocent.* I've adapted this example from one of the many excellent examples in L. Jonathan Cohen, *An Essay on Belief and Acceptance* (Oxford: Clarendon Press, 1992).

p. 112: *Psychologist Michael E. Price (like many others) has emphasized.* In "The world needs a secular community revolution," an article at the website of the Evolution Institute: https://evolution-institute.org/the-world-needs-a-secular-community-revolution/.

p. 113: *Other subgroups commonly distinguished.* See Phil Zuckerman, *Living the Secular Life: New Answers to Old Questions* (New York: Penguin Books, 2014). The labels I use are his.

p. 113: *A prominent example is the late Marcus Borg. Others are Diana Butler Bass and Brian McLaren.* For representative examples of their work, see Marcus J. Borg, *Meeting Jesus Again for the First Time: The Historical Jesus and the Heart of Contemporary Faith* (New York: HarperOne, 1995); Diana Butler Bass, *Christianity After Religion: The End of Church and the Birth of a New Spiritual Awakening* (New York: HarperOne, 2013); and Brian D. McLaren, *A New Kind of Christianity: Ten Questions That Are Transforming the Faith* (New York: HarperOne, 2010).

p. 114: *Lately, even the new atheists have gotten in on the act.* See, for example, Daniel C. Dennett, *Breaking the Spell: Religion as a Natural Phenomenon* (New York: Penguin Books, 2006), p. 205.

Chapter 10 The New Humanism

p. 117: *An excellent recent discussion and defence of secular humanism.* Philip Kitcher, *Life After Faith: The Case for Secular Humanism* (New Haven, CT: Yale University Press, 2014). Quotations in this and the following three paragraphs are taken, respectively, from pp. 61, 64, 65, 57, 59, 94, 159, and 94.

p. 119: *As the Christian philosopher George Mavrodes once charmingly put it.* George Mavrodes, "Religion and the queerness of morality," in Robert Audi and William J. Wainwright, eds., *Rationality, Religious Belief, and Moral*

Commitment: *New Essays in the Philosophy of Religion* (Ithaca, NY: Cornell University Press, 1986), p. 214.

p. 123: *As various writers, including scientists such as E. O. Wilson and James Lovelock, have told us.* I have in mind Edward O. Wilson, *Half-Earth: Our Planet's Fight for Life* (New York: Liveright, 2016) and James Lovelock, *A Rough Ride to the Future* (New York: Overlook, 2015).

p. 127: *If Charles Taylor is right in his big book A Secular Age.* Charles Taylor, *A Secular Age* (Cambridge, MA: Harvard University Press, 2007).

Epilogue: The Religion Project

p. 128: *The idea of the religion project.* This is perhaps as good a place as any to acknowledge that when I first thought of the phrase 'the religion project' and found it attractive, I was probably under the influence of another excellent book by Philip Kitcher, namely, *The Ethical Project* (Cambridge, MA: Harvard University Press, 2011).

Index

"*Religion After Science* challenges the stance held by evangelicals and atheists alike, who often assume they know the 'last word' on religious matters. What if they are both wrong, asks Schellenberg, and these are actually humankind's first, tentative words? Schellenberg is a prophet unlike any that have come before. In this highly original book, he demonstrates how the simple idea that deep time extends into the future, as well as the past, has startling consequences for today's religious debates, with the capacity to transform all of our certainties and doubts alike."

Mark Harris, Professor of Natural Science and Theology, University of Edinburgh

"A lovely book. Schellenberg makes the case that, contrary to common opinion, religion is still in a primitive stage, far from being baroquely overdeveloped. Only with time can it come into its own. As an old-fashioned non-believer, I am excited by the tussle we shall have, until one stands triumphant over the other. Read it yourself and join in the fun."

Michael Ruse, Lucyle T. Werkmeister Professor of Philosophy, Florida State University

"An impressively thoughtful and stimulating reflection on the possible future of religion, which deserves the attention of humanists and religious believers alike"

Keith Ward, Canon Professor, Christ Church Oxford

J. L. SCHELLENBERG is Professor of Philosophy at Mount Saint Vincent University, Nova Scotia. His work was honored by a special issue of the Cambridge journal *Religious Studies* in 2013.

CAMBRIDGE
UNIVERSITY PRESS
www.cambridge.org

ISBN 978-1-108-71307-8

9 781108 713078

Cover illustration: *Expect Delays* by Barbara McLean